The
I·N·D·O·O·R
Window Garden

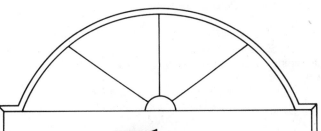

The I·N·D·O·O·R Window Garden

A guide to more than 50 beautiful and unusual plants that will flourish year-round in your home

PETER LOEWER

CB

CONTEMPORARY
BOOKS

CHICAGO

Library of Congress Cataloging-in-Publication Data

Loewer, H. Peter.
    The indoor window garden / Peter Loewer.
       p.   cm.
    Includes bibliographical references.
    ISBN 0-8092-4286-9 : $9.95
    1. Window—gardening.   2. House plants.   I. Title.
SB419.L633   1990
635.9′65—dc20   90-1619
                                          CIP

Contents

List of Illustrations

Preface

Whether it be an avocado in a pot or a bowl of forced narcissi, ever since my wife and I had our first apartment in Brooklyn, we have chosen the brightest windows for plants. Even when we lived on the dark side of Eighth Street in Manhattan and the best window was obscured most of the day by the shadow of a water tower and lines of tenements in the next block, there were philodendrons and ferns.

Then, when moving to the country, my first concern—before the leaking roof and the basement full of water—was the installation of a simple window greenhouse made of aluminum storm windows so that our eyes would have a field of green to spy before we went out to the snow and ice that crowded our Catskill Mountain winters.

Today we have a greenhouse that faces southeast (it's way too small), a sun porch that faces south (there sits a clivia that is so large I can hardly move it), and a garden that covers an acre. Yet in my studio window, snug between a laser printer on the left and a copy machine on the right, sit a loquat in a self-watering pot, some pearly moonstones, and a flamingo flower in full bloom. Once smitten with the love of plants, you become almost as bad as the bottle-cap king or the matchbook queen.

But over those years, I've garnered some favorite plants, and this book is about them. You will find odd companions such as the stapelias and the euphorbias, and beautiful ones like the amaryllis and the flowering maples, plus dozens of others that are hard to find adjectives for. I hope that you will be as excited about some of these plant discoveries as I have been and that many of them eventually find a place in your window garden.

In writing a book about houseplants, I must give special thanks to all the nurseries and growers in the country, for without their continued search for the new and loyalty to the old, there would never be enough plants to fill even the smallest of pots. An additional round of applause goes to Tovah Martin of Logee's Greenhouses and Ken Frieling and Tom Wynn of Glasshouse Works for their help in obtaining many of the plants described.

Finally, thanks must go to my agent, Dominick Abel; my editor at Contemporary Books, Bernard Shir-Cliff; and lastly to my wife, Jean, who makes everything easier by being there.

Peter Loewer
Asheville, North Carolina

Introduction

The fifty-some plants described in this book have been chosen for very personal reasons. Over the years, they have remained favorites and have earned a permanent place in my indoor garden. Some, like the wax plant, *Hoya carnosa*, are so common that they are often not listed in current plant catalogs. Others, like the Swiss-cheese plant, *Monstera deliciosa*, are considered to be so old-fashioned that many dealers call them passé. Finally, only specialty dealers would deal in such rarities as the fiberoptic plant, *Scirpus cernuus*, or an interesting ornamental grass plant like basket grass, *Oplismenus hirtellus* 'Variegatus'. But to remain popular for any length of time, a plant—like a fashion—must have staying power. I think that the plants described in this book certainly do.

As for starting an indoor garden, there are many ways to turn a window into an attractive place for plants. Shelf brackets on window jambs will hold either wooden shelves or, if the budget allows, shelves of tempered glass. A small antique table or a modern TV cart from Conran's will make a marvelous display of a number of small plants or perhaps a specimen or two in especially beautiful jardinieres. Even a window seat can become an ideal place for plants. Specialty hardware stores carry a number of elegant hooks that can be used to hold an array of hanging plants.

If the chosen window faces north, there are plants that will tolerate a low level of light, and a dim aspect can always be brightened with supplementary electric light.

A large plant in an antique pot can change the look of an entire room—at a cost much less than redoing the decor or buying a new sofa. And most variety stores and supermarkets now sell a number of potted houseplants for a reasonable sum.

Then there are all the small nurseries and greenhouses located around the country that have a larger—and often, I admit, healthier—selection of plants just waiting for a new home.

If you are a bit more adventurous, there are window greenhouses made to fit an average window opening, or you can—with a minimum amount of fuss—make your own using stock-sized aluminum storm windows from the neighborhood lumberyard or specialty store (see Appendix D).

So whatever your aspects, there is a place to start a garden in a window.

MAKING SENSE OF PLANT NAMES

Throughout this book, I have used both the common and the botanical or Latinized names for the various plants being described. This is not to confuse but to ensure that you and I are thinking of the same plants and to be certain that any plants you decide to buy are the plants that you receive from the nursery. To show that all of these botanical names have a reasonable and often delightful history behind their creation, I have, whenever possible, included the translations of the original words used in creating this often fascinating nomenclature.

Although it's true that many plants can be recognized by their common names, many more cannot. For example there are five plant genera that use "mother-in-law" in their appellations: mother-in-law or *Kalanchoe pinnata*; mother-in-law plant or *Caladium* spp. and *Dieffenbachia Seguine*; and finally mother-in-law's tongue or *Gasteria* spp., *Sansevieria trifasciata*, and *Dieffenbachia* spp. All of these names are in general use. Now imagine the local variations across the fifty states and Canada. Then picture the additional confusion when one mother-in-law plant is confused with another by someone in a nursery order department who has a migraine and hates plants to begin with. I picked this particular popular moniker not out of any disrespect but because four of the plants are included in this book.

To prevent such confusion, all known plants have been given botanical or scientific names—each unique—that are easily understood throughout the world, whatever native language is in use. In the 1700s, when the present system began, Latin was the international language of scholars and seemed the obvious choice to botanists. Most words are derived from Renaissance Latin, with a great many appropriated from ancient Greek. The man primarily thought of as the founder of the system is Carolus Linnaeus (1707–1778).

If you are concerned about pronunciation, don't be. Very few people can pronounce these names with impunity. The English, for example, have rules for Latin pronunciation that are at odds with most of the rest of the world.* Besides, you will probably use these names only in written communications.

A Guide to Names

Scientific or botanical names may contain four terms that are in general use: genus, species, variety, and cultivar (there are others, but they are beyond the scope of this book). All reference books, most gardening books, nearly all responsible catalogs and nurseries, and even the majority of seed packets list the botanical name along with the common. In many cases the common names of popular plants are really the botanical names, and people use them every day without realizing it.

---

*The English pronounce a migraine headache as meegraine and Don Juan as Don Jooan.

Delphinium, geranium, sedum, and gladiolus immediately come to mind.

In print, the genus and species are set off from the accompanying text by the use of *italics*. If the text is set in italics, the botanical name should be in roman type. All publications follow this convention except *The New York Times*, which for some reason refuses to admit its existence.

Genus refers to a group of plants that are closely related, while the *species* suggests an individual plant's unique quality, color, or even habit of growth. Either one of the names often honors the person who discovered the plant. For example, the spiderworts are called *Tradescantia* after John Tradescant, one of the greatest and most adventurous of the English plant collectors.

The genus can also be descriptive. The botanical name given to the popular spring bulb the snowdrop is *Galanthus*, from the Greek *gala*, milk, and *anthos*, flower, with milk describing the white of the flowers. The species for this flower include *byzantinus* for a type from southeast Europe, *caucasicus* for another from the Caucasus, and *grandiflorus* for one with large flowers.

The *Genus* has an initial capital and the *species* is all in lowercase letters, at least most of the time. One of the major references for botanical nomenclature used in this book is *Hortus Third*, and its authors will, on occasion, begin the species with a capital letter when it has been derived from a former generic name (name for a genus), a person's name, or a common name. I have followed that style. When referring to a species in general, the abbreviation is "spp."

The third term is variety. It is also italicized and is usually preceded by the abbreviation "var." set in roman or regular type. A variety represents a noticeable change that naturally develops in a plant by chance and breeds true from generation to generation.

The fourth term is cultivar, a term introduced in 1923 by Liberty Hyde Bailey and derived from the words *culti*vated *vari*ety. Cultivar represents a desirable variation that appears on a plant while it is in cultivation and could result either by chance or design. The word is distinguished in print usually by being set in roman type and placed inside single quotation marks. (Copyeditors take note: the last single quote appears before a period or comma.) Some references delete the single quotes and precede the cultivar name with cv.

It should be noted that many plants listed in catalogs have botanical names that are woefully out of date. This is because the catalog writers know that the public recognizes, for example, the name *Lisianthus* but will be unfamiliar with the current and correct name of *Eustoma*, so they use the old. I've indicated both names when possible.

CARE AND FEEDING OF THE PLANTS

With every plant described in this book are instructions for care that include light requirements, the proper soil mix, when and how to water, when to fertilize, and how to propagate. Rather than using tables to provide this information, I have included it with every plant entry.

LIGHT

When writing about some light requirements, I've used the term *footcandle*. A footcandle (FC) is the amount of light cast on a white surface by one candle, one foot away, in an otherwise dark room. You can get an idea of the light intensity your plants are receiving by using the exposure meter on a regular camera for measurements. Set the film speed to ASA 200, the shutter speed to 1/500 of a second,

and adjust the f-stop, then take the reading using a piece of white cardboard until the meter gives the OK.

$$
\begin{array}{rcl}
f22 & = & 5,000 \text{ FC} \\
f16 & = & 2,500 \text{ FC} \\
f11 & = & 1,200 \text{ FC} \\
f8 & = & 550 \text{ FC} \\
f6.3 & = & 300 \text{ FC} \\
f4.5 & = & 150 \text{ FC}
\end{array}
$$

Plants that need full sun, such as most cactuses and flowering plants, generally require 6,000 to 8,000 FC. Begonias and many jungle-born houseplants prefer partial shade or an average of 2,000 FC. Deep-jungle dwellers like 250 to 500 FC. Many plants will survive 20 FC for a few weeks, with 50 FC being a bit better, but 100 FC seems to be the minimum needed for growth and sustaining life.

Speaking of light, windows lose light through outside refraction of the glass and the absorption of some light by the glass itself. Architectural details like eaves and cornices mean the loss of more light. A west window, for example, in midmorning may read 400 FC at the inside sill, but only 10 FC when measured six feet into the room, while outside the light will produce 10,000 FC. A thin layer of dust on the tops of houseplants further cuts down on the light received by plant cells, so remember to periodically dust and wash your plants right along with Aunt Ethel's Chinese porcelain vase and Uncle Herbert's portrait. You can read a newspaper with 50 FC, but it's hardly enough to keep a plant alive, much less healthy.

SOIL MIXES FOR POTTING THE PLANTS

All of the plants in this book have specific likes and dislikes when it comes to soil mixes. For all of them I have given simple recipes that include recommendations using a good commercial potting soil, peat moss, sphagnum moss, composted manure, and sharp sand.

Commercial potting soil is usually sold in ten- and twenty-pound bags at nursery centers and variety stores. It should be labeled as being sterilized, or don't buy it—the eventual germination of the weed seeds in an unsterilized mix will drive you mad.

Peat moss is partially decomposed sphagnum moss that is excellent to loosen soil. Sphagnum moss identifies several different kinds of mosses that grow in bogs and swamps (apparently more in Canada than anywhere else). Since it's sterile, it's extensively used for the germination of seedlings and as a growing medium for bog plants.

Composted manure (either sheep or cow) is usually for sale in twenty- and forty-pound bags and is easier (and neater) to use than regular animal manure.

Sand is one of the main constituents of a good soil, making a heavy soil porous. Use builder's sand or sharp sand, being sure to wash it before use. "Sharp" simply means that the sand grains are rough to the touch, as opposed to soft sand, which is generally too fine to be useful. Beach sand is too full of salt and is also soft.

FERTILIZERS

The composted manure added to the various soil mixes will usually provide sufficient nutrients for most plants if they are repotted annually. But if a plant is a heavy feeder and is submitted to continual waterings, nutrients will soon be leached from the soil, and the plants will suffer. So in the text I have suggested periodic applications of liquid fertilizer.

If you are in an organic frame of mind, use one of the fish emulsion concentrates. These are natural, nonburning formulas derived from seagoing fish. Be sure to buy the deodorized products, especially if you plan on using them indoors.

Other liquid fertilizers can be used without any worry on the gardener's part. Some come in a concentrate with a medicine-stopper top for easy mixing, and others are in powder form and must be dissolved in tepid water. Just follow package directions.

POTS IN GENERAL

Believe it or not, aesthetics can enter into the indoor garden. Usually the way in revolves around pots. I, for one, object to plastic pots. The simple plastic pot in dark green certainly has its place when used for seedlings or as a liner for a fancy container, but when they are manufactured to mimic clay or are decorated with sleeping Mexicans for succulent use or cute little cats or coy little dogs for African violets, my psyche gets upset.

So the majority of my pots are clay. Clay will allow plant roots to breathe; air flows in and out of the tiny pores found within the clay wall of a pot. Using such a pot provides a safety margin especially since people tend to overwater rather than underwater plants. If fertilizer salts in the form of a white crust build up on pot rims—usually from the continual leaching of water—I scrape it off with the edge of a knife or wait for repotting, when a metal scrub brush or a heavy-duty scouring pad will do the job.

Pot Size

For choosing a pot, the rules of proportion come into play. When the plant is in correct proportion to the pot, the whole affair looks properly balanced. In the

Brooklyn Botanic Garden's *Indoor Gardening*, Elvin McDonald writes:

> The rule of thumb I use is this: let the size of the pot equal one-half to one-third the height or width of the plant, depending on whether it is primarily vertical or horizontal. This suggests a 6-inch pot for an angel-wing begonia [that is] 12 to 18 inches tall, a 4-inch pot for an African violet that measures 8 inches across.

Self-Watering Pots

Pots that feature reservoirs to hold additional water have been on the market for a decade or so. They allow you to provide moisture-loving plants with just the proper amount of water without getting the soil or the plant roots too wet. They are also great for taking care of plants while you are on a short vacation.

In addition, you can purchase water wicks to draw water from a nearby container into the soil to meet your plant's demands. You can also make your own water wicks out of strips of fiberglass or cotton wicks from kerosene lamps. Bury the free end of the wick into a reservoir of water. Capillary action draws the water up through the wick to keep the soil evenly moist.

WATERING PLANTS

When it comes to watering, the mistakes made by gardeners are legion. And since water is the lifeblood of a plant, such mistakes are often fatal.

No single set of instructions can cover every aspect of watering, since the evaporation or absorption of water depends on the type of soil, the type of pot, the heat of the day, and the kind of root system the plant possesses.

Roots, for example, come in many varieties. Begonias have thin, fibrous roots that quickly perish if allowed to dry out, while most of the succulents have thick roots that can take a great deal of punishment.

In the plant descriptions, I have given individual instructions for watering in order to help the grower with this vexing problem. And whenever possible I have recommended using self-watering pots.

Transplanting

Just as an iceberg is largely under water, much of a plant is beneath the soil and consists of roots. Surprisingly enough, the major part of a root is never really seen, for on these roots are very tiny root hairs. These root hairs are tiny projections that become completely enmeshed in the soil, and when the plant is repotted, they are often ripped from the parent root. Although this is not a problem with succulents, most transplants quickly wilt. Luckily root hairs grow quickly, and the plant usually recovers.

The shock of transplanting can usually be minimized by moving as much as possible of the original soil that surrounds the roots. After transplanting, it's a good idea to spray additional water on the leaves and to cover the plant for a few days with a piece of plastic wrap to serve as a miniature high-humidity greenhouse.

PROPAGATION

If buyers had to wait for suppliers to grow from seed all the plants people want, there would never be enough plants to go around. Luckily, nature has accomplished an alternative method called asexual or vegetative reproduction, which leads to the manufacture of thousands of clones to meet consumer demand. For a list of the best ways to reproduce 179 different houseplants, see Appendix C.

Softwood Cuttings

The term *softwood* refers to the soft, green stem tissues found in houseplant annuals or the first season's growth of perennials before the stem matures into woody tissue.

Late spring and early summer are the best time to propagate with softwood cuttings. If you want only a few plants, I've found the best method is a combination of peat pots or Jiffy-7s and small plastic food bags. First choose a plant that needs pruning. Cut the healthy stems, which are about three to six inches long, with a sharp knife or razor blade slightly below the point where a leaf petiole (or stalk) joins the stem. Remove any damaged leaves and flowers, and neatly slice off any bottom leaves close to the stem. Take an expanded Jiffy pot (any small container will do), and make a hole in the medium with a pencil or similar object at three-quarters of the pot's depth. Insert the cutting, making sure that the base of the stem touches the bottom of the hole. Firm the medium back into place around the stem. Now put the whole affair in a small plastic bag with the opening at the top.

If the air is very dry, seal the bag with a twist. The bag holds the moisture that the leaves throw off but cannot replace until new roots form. The medium should be moist at all times, but never soggy! Plastic bags that are sealed should be opened every few days and checked for mold. The stagnant air and damp conditions give mold and fungus a helping hand.

In about two weeks, give the cuttings a slight tug to check whether rooting has commenced. If not, pull out the cuttings, and see whether the end has started to rot. If all looks well, try again, perhaps dusting with one of the hormone powders. Make doubly sure that the base of the cutting is touching the rooting medium; it needs the stimulus of this contact to start new roots.

Hormones

Plant cells resemble animal cells in many ways, including that both use hormones to control and stimulate growth and development. Often, a cutting that refuses to respond to the rooting process simply needs the additional stimulation of a plant-growth hormone. Dip cuttings from vigorous plants in the powder, using pieces between three and six inches long. Remove any flowers or leaves at the base of the cutting. Make sure there are no air pockets around the stem end. Hormone powders should be used with care, as they can cause skin irritation.

Sectioned-Leaf Cuttings

Sansevieria and other common houseplants can be reproduced by sectioning a leaf. Cut a healthy leaf into pieces, each three or four inches long. This process will not work if the leaf is upside down, so make the bottom cut on a slant just to keep directions straight. Plant three inches of the cutting in a rooting medium, like moist sphagnum or sand. A new plant will develop to one side of the mother leaf.

Single-Leaf Cuttings

Streptocarpus, gloxinias, African violets, hoyas, and many other plants can be reproduced by using variations of a single leaf, leaf with petiole, or the leaf, the petiole, and a section of the stem including the bud.

When using leaves that are thick, waxy, and of a succulent character, the cuttings need not be covered, but be sure the medium stays moist.

Cuttings in Water

An old-time method of propagation is rooting cuttings in a glass of water. It works for ivies, begonias, inch plants, and many more.

One thing to remember is to change the water every few days, to give new oxygen to the plant. If water remains unchanged, the rooting will usually occur near the water's surface, where oxygen is more plentiful, and there won't be enough new growth to support the plant.

After roots have shown healthy growth, add small amounts of sand or soil to the water every few days. You won't have a tangled mass of roots to sort out when ready to transplant, and the soil or sand will stimulate the roots to grow new root hairs, which are the true providers of food and water to a plant.

Plants by Division

Another easy way to produce new plants is by division of the root stock. Early spring is the best time, before new growth begins for the coming season. This process works with plants that form multiple crowns, and it obviously will not work for a single-stemmed plant.

Runners

Any houseplants that produce runners with tiny plants at their tips will make new plants if the tips are allowed to root. The easiest way is to use a bobby pin or a paper clip to anchor the small plant to a three-inch pot of soil. Make sure that adequate roots have formed by giving a slight tug before you cut the runner from the mother plant.

GROWING PLANTS FROM SEED

One of the best ways to expand a houseplant collection is to start new plants from seed. Not only is it relatively inexpensive, it's always more enjoyable to grow your own seedlings; there's a certain excitement in seeing the first touch of green pushing up through the soil, knowing that you provided the necessary environment for the seed to germinate.

The Best Season

Try to buy and start your seeds in early spring. Take full advantage of the long growing season ahead. Although some plants many be initiated at any time of the year (see Appendix C), the majority profit from matching their growth with the lengthening days of spring.

Try, too, not to be smitten with the lovely pictures in catalogs. Limit your buying to what you have room and equipment for, remembering that your time is valuable. Endless trays, all with emerging plants, can be an awesome responsibility.

One of the most important things to remember when starting seeds is to use a sterile medium so your seedlings never have problems with a killing fungus called "damping off." Any of the major seed companies have special mixes you can purchase by the bag.

All of today's seed packets come with complete instructions on how deep to plant the seed, whether the seed needs light in order to germinate, and how to water once germination has begun.

Five Rules for Proper Germination

To make sure that your plants germinate properly, follow these rules:

1 Don't overwater, since you deprive the seed of needed oxygen.
2 Never let the growing mix dry out; once the germination process begins, seeds

must have a constant supply of moisture.

3 When watering with a watering can, use a mister or a rose, since the full force of water can damage fragile seedlings.

4 Never sow seeds too deeply. If in doubt, just cover them lightly.

5 Keep seeds from direct sunlight until germination is complete.

PESTS IN THE OUTBACK

Once aphids have made a beachhead in your indoor garden, they tend to appear with the regularity of bubbles in a Lava Lamp. But bad as they are, at least you can spot an aphid as it sluggishly sucks the sap from fresh young leaves and stems. So, in my gardening world, spider mites are even worse: They are such tiny creepers that most of us miss their presence until their numbers and the webs they produce multiply to the point where leaves brown and shrivel, looking as though each is wrapped in the most delicate of webbing. By this stage it's usually too late to save the plant.

The only person who could ever have faced either of these creatures head on is the incredible shrinking man, that hero of an existential sci-fi movie of the sixties, but the scriptwriters—knowing how much an audience can take—confronted our hero with a cat when he was two feet tall, an average house spider when he had shrunk to an inch, and left aphids and mites out of the cast.

I have had infestations of both these pests, aphids usually in the spring and spider mites first appearing either during the dog days of August when the heat is high and the humidity low—they love desert conditions—and I've been so busy out-of-doors that I've neglected my houseplants or later when plants that have been outside are once again brought indoors.

Aphids

Aphids usually time their arrival to those days in the spring when your seedlings have started to stretch their new leaves to the lights above or the sun shining through a window. The perfection of an aphid's reproductive system is such that a female aphid will mate in the fall, laying eggs on a vacationing houseplant that you then bring indoors—just like a Trojan horse—where the eggs spend the winter and hatch in the spring. The resulting insects are all females that are known by the wonderful term *stem mothers*. These ladies of the stem then produce several generations of offspring asexually; only this time they don't bother with the egg business, but bear their offspring alive. These children of the stem are either born without wings and just stay around in the neighborhood and eat, or are born with wings and then fly to greener pastures, in this case your emergent seedlings. Soon both the stay-at-homes and the fly-by-nights are involved in producing more aphids. And don't underestimate this insect's production capabilities. Ten days after an aphid is born, this virgin daughter is not only eating away but at the same time is producing more aphids, once again born alive.

Not only do these insects weaken a plant, their feeding can distort leaves and flower petals, and their excrement (which has a high sugar content) can give rise to mildew and also attract ants.

Spider Mites

But aphids are in the minor leagues when compared to the spider mite, truly one of nature's most awesome and awful creatures. Spider mites love heat, and as cold weather arrives they can actually invade your home, either by migration or by hitching a ride on a houseplant that has been outside for the summer. And remember, all the time they are engaged in this search for heat, they are laying eggs, so plants in the garden are already harboring next year's plagues.

If your house is warm and dry—as most houses are—the mites soon show up as tiny specks wandering the undersurface of a leaf, where females spin loose webs to hold their eggs, and males protect unmated females from other male competition by shooting silk in an attempt to tie them down; there is no parthenogenesis here. In this drama, the combatants are less than one thirty-second of an inch long. Once they become established, the female lays about one hundred eggs during a two-week cycle, and each egg will soon hatch and produce another hundred, all hungry.

The mites are motionless as they, like the aphids, suck the life juices of a plant. But if disturbed, they quickly race about their webbing, looking for a port in the storm. If you place a piece of white paper under the infected leaves and then shake the leaf, the mites will fall and be easy to see rushing about on the paper's surface.

Defenses

Of the two, I'd much rather fight an aphid infestation, because you can—if the invasion is limited—wallow in your rage and crush them by rubbing the infected leaf or stem between your index finger and thumb and generally see the results. Spider mites are more difficult because they are so small that you're never sure you've gotten them all. By the time the indoor gardener sees the problem, it's usually on its way to being out of control, so other measures are needed.

Whatever the pest involved, the first step is to remove your plant from the company of others, keeping it apart until there is no more evidence of infection. When the problem is aphids and the weather is still clement, take the plant outside. During the winter, move it to the sink or tub and, using the outside hose, faucet, or a shower hose—and humming a tune from *South Pacific*—wash the aphids away. They have a tenuous grasp on plant stems and can easily be dislodged. I do not own a leaf blower, but it would be interesting to know whether a blast of air would dislodge them as easily as a blast of water.

For a light dose of spider mites, first cover the pot's soil with a sheet of aluminum foil, so the soil will not spill out. Using a bar of white hand soap or one of the new insecticidal soaps, lather up and completely cover both sides of the leaves and the stems with soapsuds. If the leaves are tender, use your fingers; if the leaves are tougher, a small brush will do no harm. After the suds sit on the leaves for a few minutes, carefully rinse them off and return the plant to isolation, renewing the attack in a week. Wash the plant a second time even if you see no immediate sign of mites; there is still the possibility of hatching eggs. Be patient—perseverance will pay off.

Insecticidal Soaps

If infestations are light, you can spray the plant with insecticidal soaps, making sure you read the label first. This is important because a few plants like palms or some members of the Euphorbia family will be damaged by the soap. If ferns are infected, increase the recommended dilution. With soap in your arsenal, there is no need to resort to chemical sprays, bombs, or whatever. The potential health risk to you, your family, and your pets is not worth the effort. Beware of any pesticide that gives you a toll-free number to call in case of accident.

Scale and Mealybugs

Believe it or not, shellac is made from a

scale insect found in India. This is the only good thing I've ever heard about this group of insects. When young, they are too tiny and colorless to be noticed as they walk up a stem while searching for a good leaf for personal attachment. When settled down, they develop a thick, armored hide and literally glue themselves to the leaf surface and begin to eat. You can flick them off with your fingernail, but a cleaner method is swabbing them off with a cotton Q-Tip soaked in alcohol.

Mealybugs are other common pests. Closely related to scale, they resemble small mounds of cotton fluff. Use the Q-Tip and alcohol solution for control. If they attack the roots of succulents, remove the plants from the infected soil, then dip the roots in alcohol, rinse well, and replant in fresh soil.

Commonsense Rules

Here are five commonsense rules that will go a long way in protecting your plants:

1 Quarantine new plants for at least two weeks. Most pests will show up by then.
2 Keep all plant debris picked up. Don't allow piles of organic litter to accumulate and become a potential breeding ground for trouble.
3 Keep leaves clean and dust-free, examining the plants while cleaning to spot potential troublemakers.
4 No matter how fond you are of your plant, if the infestation is too far gone, destroy the plant and the soil.
5 Give all plants a thorough inspection after their summer outside before they join others in your collection.

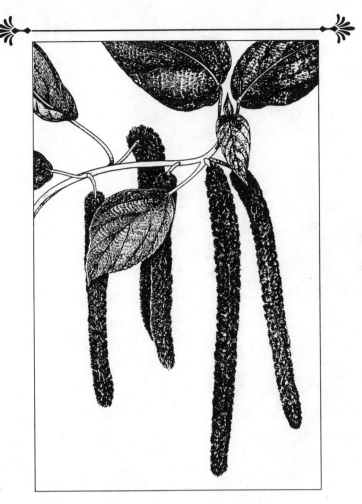

PART ONE

PLANTS FOR FLOWERS OR FRUIT

The following plants have been selected mainly because they have attractive or beautiful flowers or produce fruit. That doesn't mean the leaves aren't worth the growing. Many of the flowering maples or the begonias would be worth having if only for the leaves alone, the flowers becoming an extra bonus. And wait until you see a well-grown kalanchoe. . . .

The Flowering Maple

We've had a flowering maple in our window since the days that we lived in a five-flight walk-up in Manhattan back in the late sixties. The plants are extremely popular for pots, as they flower over a long period of time and can also spend productive summers in the garden as splendid bedding plants.

The generic name is *Abutilon*, an Arabic name for a species of mallow, which these flowers closely resemble. The common name refers to the shape of the leaf, for they closely resemble maple leaves both in size and in shape.

One species, *Abutilon Theophrasti*, known variously as the velvetleaf, the butter-print, the pie-marker, or China jute, is a naturalized wildflower—often called weedy—found growing across the United States and considered an important fiber plant in northern China. The whole plant is velvety with single inch-wide yellow flowers and an unusually shaped fruit that is often used in dried-flower arrangements.

But those grown in windows are usually called *Abutilon hybridum*, a species that has given rise to an unusual number of hybrids of many colors and qualities that bloom for most of the year. Flower colors include coral pink, deep red, deep rose, pure white, lemon yellow, and orange.

Plants can be set outside after frost danger is past and bloom throughout the summer, wanting only a spot in full or partial sun and plenty of water. Then, as fall approaches, they can be dug up, put back into pots, and pruned back by at least two-thirds; they proceed to bloom in a sunny window for most of the winter. At least five hours of sun and night temperatures of 50°–60°F are needed for the best winter flowers. When plants are not flowering during the winter, it's best to keep the soil almost dry, with just enough water to prevent wilting of the leaves.

Seeds may be started in February or March with a soil temperature of 60°F. Pot the seedlings when four to six leaves have appeared, using a soil of potting soil, peat moss, and sand, one-third each. A mature plant is happy in a seven-inch pot. Since the plant can get scraggly, remember to pinch it back in the early spring. Cuttings from old wood can be taken in September.

Plants should be fertilized every two or three weeks throughout the summer and benefit particularly from fish emulsions.

Abutilon megapotamicum, or the trailing abutilon, is from Brazil and will survive outdoors in the far South and southern California. 'Variegata' is an especially fine cultivar with yellow-and-green mottled foliage and yellow flowers with a red calyx, perfectly suited for growing in hanging baskets.

Abutilon pictum 'Thompsonii' is originally from Brazil and bears bright orange flowers with mottled yellow-and-green foliage. The leaf colors in this case are caused by a transmissible virus, for if a variegated shoot is grafted on a green-leafed stock, the whole plant soon becomes variegated. This particular plant is also a good subject for becoming a standard tree. Start with a small plant of only one shoot and pot it in a three-inch pot, tying the stem to a foot-long bamboo cane or stick that you have inserted in the dirt at the pot's edge. Use one loop of soft cord about the stem and one loop on the stake so the stem is never crushed. When the flowering maple grows to about ten inches, move it to a six-inch pot, adding a longer stake. Now remove all the side shoots, leaving just one at the tip of the stem.

As the plant approaches two feet, move it to an eight-inch pot—remember, all the time you have been forcing the plant upward, the roots have been growing, too. Now pinch off the terminal bud to force

The Flowering Maple
Abutilon pictum 'Thompsonii'

the plant into bushy growth. The stem will develop a woody look, and you will have a beautiful flowering tree.

The Willow-Leaved Acacia

I completely forgot to water my pot of willow-leaved acacia during a spell of hot weather earlier this summer. The pot hangs on a runner, and the runner is overhead, with the plant's branches arching out over a foot on either side of the pot's edge. When I saw browning leaves, I realized my error and ran for the watering can. Within two weeks, new leaves were appearing, and I never lost a blossom.

Acacias are tough plants that number some eight hundred species, with most of them coming from Australia, where they are called wattles. The botanical name is from the Greek *akakia* and originally meant a thorny tree found in the deserts of Egypt.

My plant is *Acacia retinodes*, known in Australia as the wirilda or sometimes the monthly mimosa, this last name because the small flowers are produced from early March right through to November. In nature the plant becomes a small tree, reaching a height of twenty feet, and is hardy in the south of England. Many trees are grown for decoration along the French Riviera.

Pizzetti and Cocker, in their marvelous book *Flowers: A Guide for Your Garden*, report that the wirilda was introduced from the Australian state of Victoria to Europe in 1656. Mine arrived last year and began as a rooted cutting—acacia cuttings of half-ripened shoots are slow to root but not difficult. It bloomed right away, bearing dozens of tiny, fragrant yellow balls, each beginning at a diameter of a sixteenth of an inch and ending up about a quarter of an

inch across. Other acacias are found on the market and known for bigger flowers, but this particular plant is among the toughest around. It's often used as grafting stock for less hardy varieties.

Propagation is usually by seed, and germination is accelerated by softening the hard seed coats, either by placing them in hot ashes and allowing them to cool or by dropping seeds in boiling water and leaving them to soak in the cooling water until the seed coats are inflated, a process taking about four days.

Use a potting mix of one-half potting soil and one-half peat moss. Keep the soil on the dry side, and try for a winter temperature of 50°–55°F. Indoors give them as much light as possible, and let plants spend the summer outdoors in full sun. Fertilize once a month during the warmer part of the year.

The Chenille Plant

Everblooming is a term that is thrown about with great abandon by many members of the horticultural world, especially those who sell flowering plants. But few are the plants that produce flowers for months—not to mention years—on end. Among those plants that will perform is the chenille plant or, as it's sometimes called, red-hot cattails, foxtail, or the Philippine Medusa. First introduced from New Guinea in the late 1800s, this tropical shrub is so proficient a bloomer that even a rooted cutting will soon produce flowers.

The botanical name is *Acalypha hispida*. The genus was first used by Hippocrates to describe the nettle, which the red flowers of this plant somewhat resemble, and *hispida* is from the Latin for bristly.

I never thought it would number among my favored plants, as the blossoms do resemble a type of bedspread fabric

Willow-Leaved Acacia
Acacia retinodes ▶

called chenille (from the French for caterpillar) often found in very cheap motels. But the quality of bloom is so exciting that I succumbed, and it now is one of my favorites.

There is a cultivar called 'Alba', which bears creamy white flowers with a flush of pink that intensifies during the summer months.

Give the plant a sunny window (except in midsummer), keep the soil evenly moist (this plant is a good candidate for a self-watering pot), and never allow temperatures to fall below 60°F, and your plant will soon develop its flowers up to a foot long. Soil should be one-quarter each of a good potting soil, peat moss, composted manure, and sand. Feed the plant every month during warm weather. Propagate by stem cuttings with a heel in the spring to have plants blooming for fall.

They are subject to spider mites, so make sure you mist the leaves every day, and look under the leaves on occasion just to be sure you haven't been invaded.

If happy, plants can become quite large, as they are shrubs in the tropics.

The Amaryllis or Hippeastrum

Over the years of being a garden writer, I have been asked more questions on how to keep amaryllis in bloom from year to year than any other single houseplant problem. The biggest hurdle that I see is the mistaken belief that this plant is a bulb that should be allowed to become dormant for at least half of the year.

To begin with, the amaryllis is a more or less evergreen plant that arises from a bulb. Nursery suppliers and many growers allow the bulbs to dry off after flowering, both for convenience in the greenhouse and for the ease of shipping dormant bulbs to market. In fact, seedling plants should never be dried off until they reach flowering size. If properly cared for, your amaryllis will become larger every year and will continue to flower with increasing vigor and blatant display.

There is confusion even with botanical nomenclature, for many people still believe that *Amaryllis* is the correct generic name for this popular winter houseplant. Well, it is a generic name, but for a genus with but one species—an entirely different bulbous plant known as the belladonna lily or *Amaryllis Belladonna*. The confusion arose in the United States because growers did not want to confuse the American consumer with the correct name, *Hippeastrum*.

The genus *Hippeastrum* contains some seventy-five species, mostly native to tropical America (one hails from Africa), and is sometimes called the equestrian star-flower. This last name comes from *hippeus*, or knight on horseback, and *astron*, a star. Why? Nobody really knows, for—like many names in the botanical world—the initial reasoning is lost in the mists of time.

The bulbs can be left out-of-doors in the southern tip of Florida, a bit of southern Texas (where it touches Mexico and the Gulf), and a few small areas of California. Elsewhere this is a potted houseplant with a sojourn to the backyard during the heat of summer.

Hippeastrum vittatum was first introduced from the Chilean Andes in 1769 and bore strap-shaped leaves and up to six six-inch wide flowers of white with a magenta stripe. One watchmaker in England, by the name of Arthur Johnson, crossed this plant with *H. reginae*—the one plant from Africa—and produced the first hybrid, now called *Hippeastrum × Johnsonii*, or St. Joseph's lily, a bulb that produced three or four tubular flowers of brilliant scarlet streaked with white.

Chenille Plant
Acalypha hispida

Using this plant as a starter, Dutch hybridizers have produced the 'Leopoldii Hybrid' bulbs that bear flowers of almost all colors except blue. So today when you see an amaryllis advertised for home or greenhouse, it's usually a descendant of one of these plants.

Sometimes an entirely new bulb appears on the plant horizon. The butterfly amaryllis (*Hippeastrum papilion*) is described as having a blossom 5½ inches high and 3½ inches wide with a background color of white, lightly touched with soft green and having crimson-maroon markings radiating from the throat.

As for the lack of a blue flower, for years horticulturists and nurserypeople have touted the fabulous blue amaryllis, *Hippeastrum procerum*, but this turns out to be *Worsleya Rayneri*, a one-species genus from Brazil. This long-necked bulb was named after Arthington Worsley (1861–1943), a mining engineer who traveled extensively in South America.

To plant an amaryllis, fill a pot two-thirds full with a soil mix of one-quarter each of potting soil, peat moss, composted manure, and sand. Choose a pot no larger than two inches more than the bulb's diameter. Bury the bulb in the soil, but leave the top part (about one-quarter) uncovered. Keep the soil moist but not wet, and set the pot in a warm spot.

After the leaves appear, feed the plant every month during active growth, and allow at least four hours of full sun with 50°F at night and 70°F during the day. Every summer after the first year, replace the top inch of soil with fresh, and pot on every third year. In time a healthy bulb can produce many flowers and attain a circumference of some fourteen inches. After the nights are warm and frost danger is past, you can place the potted bulbs out in the garden for the summer.

From late October to mid-December,

keep the bulb slightly drier and allow a rest. When you wish to start a bloom, bring the pot into a warm place. When the flower stalk is some six inches high, place the plant in a sunny window.

If you wish to store the bulbs, in September withhold water completely and allow the leaves to turn yellow and die back. When they are completely brown, cut them off at the top of the bulb. Dormant bulbs and pots are best stored on their sides in a place with temperatures no lower than 40°F. To start flowering, add water and bring to a warm room.

Remove the flowers after blossoming is completed, unless you wish to set seed. Don't worry about the water that seeps out of the sheared stalk. It will soon stop.

Amaryllis from Seed

Cross-pollinating your own amaryllis hybrids is a fascinating hobby. Try to pick two parents of pure color—a red with another shade of red or bright orange with a dark orange—since hybridizers say this gives the best results. Using a small, clean watercolor brush, take pollen from the anthers of one flower and brush some on the stigma of the second. Separate the recipient plant, and remove its anthers so no other pollen is involved.

When the pods ripen and burst, black seeds will appear, stacked like slices of bread. Sow these seeds in sphagnum moss or a good prepared mix, covering them lightly. Using a germination temperature of 60°–65°F, seeds should germinate within ten to fifteen days. When seedlings are old enough to handle, place ten in a six-inch pot, and keep them in a warm place.

When the leaves are six inches long, pot each plant individually in a four-inch pot, using the recommended mix. Remember, until they flower for the first time, never let them dry out.

◀ Amaryllis
Amaryllis 'Leopoldii Hybrid'

Be sure to keep accurate records of your trials and errors.

The Flamingo Flower

J.-K. Huysmans (1848–1907) was a French novelist born of a Dutch family who is today remembered for having written the book that Dorian Gray—in Oscar Wilde's masterpiece—claimed "was the strangest book he had ever read."

The title was *A Rebours* or, in English, *Against the Grain*. Its hero, Des Esseintes, was a young Parisian who spent his life trying to realize in the nineteenth century all the passions, philosophies, and modes of thought that were found in every previous age except his own.

"After such a book," wrote Barbey d'Aurevilly, the famous author of *Les Diaboliques*, "there remains nothing left for the Author but to choose between the jaw of a pistol or the foot of the Cross." Quite a statement about a book written in 1884.

But what has all this to do with flowering plants?

Des Esseintes was passionately interested in flowers but was most delighted by "rare plants of high-bred type, coming from distant lands, kept alive by skill and pains in an artificial equatorial temperature maintained by carefully regulated furnaces." And for a time his greatest joy of all was keeping an artificial flower that aped the true. But toward the end of the book, he truly wished for natural flowers that imitated the false:

[The nurseryman] unloaded a tangled mass of leaves, lozenge-shaped, bottle-green in hue; from the midst rose a switch on top of which trembled a great ace of hearts, as smooth and shiny as a capsicum; then, as if to defy all the familiar aspects of plants, from the middle of this ace of hearts, of an intense vermilion, sprang a flesh tail, downy, white and yellow, upright in some case, corkscrewed above the heart, like a pig's tail, in others.

It was, of course, an anthurium.

The botanical name is also *Anthurium* from the Latin *anthos*, flower, and *oura*, tail. They are tropical plants from South America and number some six hundred species. In most of them, a single blossom with the consistency of patent leather and dyed in various shades of red—not really a petal but a spathe, or modified leaf—wraps itself around a spadix, a column covered with numerous tiny flowers, male on the top and female on the bottom. The dozens of tiny flowers are clearly seen only when examined under a magnifying glass.

Anthuriums must have a humid and warm atmosphere at all times. Never let temperatures fall below 60°F. They like morning sun but should be protected from hot afternoon sun, as they mostly come from deep jungles. A mix of one-quarter each of potting soil, peat moss, composted manure, and sand is best, and the plants do well in self-watering pots, as the soil should always be evenly moist.

The plants are climbers and will eventually lift themselves above the pot. Wrap the new roots in moist sphagnum moss, and eventually you can repot the plant up to the level of the new bottom leaf.

At present I have *Anthurium scherzeranum* 'Rothschildianum', an extravagant cultivar with a large spathe of creamy white dotted with red specks and a very curly spadix of sulphur yellow. It is definitely a conversation piece. The blooms last for weeks before they eventually expire.

Other types include *Anthurium radicans*,

Flamingo
Anthurium scherzeranum 'Rothschildianum' ▶

a prostrate creeping dwarf with metallic leaves; *A. scandens* with shiny foliage and small green flowers with a little spathe and a longer spadix; and *A. Andraeanum* 'Mickey Mouse', another dwarf hybrid with shiny scarlet flowers that have earlike lobes.

Propagation is by division, making sure each new plant has a separate crown. Many new hybrids are available by seed. Colors include various shades of orange, pink, white, and red. Only fresh seed will germinate, but most suppliers take orders for anthurium seed, so freshness is guaranteed. Seed should be sown in damp sphagnum moss, slightly covered, and placed in a moist, propagating case with a temperature of 75°–85°F. Germination takes up to thirty days, but often considerably longer.

The Beefsteak Begonia

The begonia is both the common name and the generic name for a large collection of mostly tropical plants that have given rise to one of the most popular summer bedding plants, the annual *Begonia semperflorens* hybrids; truly beautiful hanging basket plants, the tuberous begonias; and a number of fanciful cultivars with glorious leaves, including the time-honored rex begonia.

The generic name *Begonia* was verified by Linnaeus in 1724 but first used by one Charles Plumier, a Franciscan monk, in honor of Michel Bégon (1638–1710), at one time the intendant of the French Antilles and eventually Canada, who was an avid amateur botanist and plant collector. Earlier Georg Rumpf (1628–1702) described begonias from the islands located between New Guinea and the Celebes, and it's fortunate his name was not honored, or we would be growing flowering rumpfs in our backyards.

For a number of years I had many pots of begonias, chiefly *Begonia* 'Queen Mother' and *Begonia* 'Iron Cross' and a number of smaller specimens, but invariably I would forget to keep them warm, or for some other reason they would start to be less than attractive. So I would always wind up giving them away to various visitors over the garden year.

Sometimes I would plant seed of *Begonia semperflorens* cultivars, starting in June in order to have flowering plants in December. But even that activity gave way to a fascination with more exotic plants.

But there is one begonia in our collection of plants that has been growing and blooming—on and on and on—since my sister-in-law brought it over some fifteen years ago. It's an old-fashioned beefsteak or pondleaf begonia (*Begonia* × *erythrophylla*) and was taken from a cutting provided by her mother plant, which is at least sixty years old and belonged to an aunt on her husband's side of the family— and the years roll by.

I've got it now in a large self-watering pot (it measures a foot square), and the stem (or, more correctly, the rhizome) has twirled around and around itself in such a complicated configuration that I continually hesitate to repot it, an activity that it sorely needs. For a houseplant companion to go on year after year with a minimum of care is something of a rarity. (When the picture was drawn, it was still in a clay pot.)

The leathery and rounded leaves are a highly polished green with maroon undersides. The plant flowers freely with lovely pink flowers, usually in February, and it enjoys evenly moist soil and morning or afternoon sun with temperatures that fluctuate between 50° and 65°F. I use the usual potting soil, peat moss, and sand mix, one-third each, and try to remember to fertilize at least once a month during the summer, but often forget.

Beefsteak Begonia ▶
Begonia × *erythrophylla*

The plant propagates freely from cuttings taken in spring.

ANOTHER GREAT BEGONIA

There is another stellar begonia in my collection of window houseplants. It's called a shrub begonia, and the botanical name is *Begonia* 'Alleryi'. This is a cultivar derived from a crossing of *B. gigantea* and *B. metallica* by one Allery Aubert back in 1904.

While reading *The Adventurous Gardener*, I had seen a color illustration of a begonia in a collection of pot plants on Christopher Lloyd's front porch. Included in the group were a fall-blooming lily, *Lilium formosanum* (he notes that it's deliciously scented and the earwigs come out at night to feed on its pollen, which shows the English predilection for being kind to anything, including the repulsive earwig) and a pink-leaved begonia called *Begonia haageana*, said to gain that coloring if starved.

It turns out that *Begonia haageana* is also an incorrect name for a cultivar of obscure origins developed in 1939 from a hybridization that included one known parent, *B. Scharffii*, and is now called 'Drostii'. The nursery I ordered the plant from was out of the second and sent me the first, and I've never been sorry.

These particular begonias are also known as hirsute or hairy-leaved begonias and are among the easiest to grow in the entire family. They need watering only when dry, and they prefer a shady eastern or western exposure with a temperature above 50°F at night.

'Alleryi' can reach a height of five feet if grown well. The entire plant is covered with silky and short white hairs. Leaves are deeply cut and pointed, a glossy green on top and pale green with maroon veins on the bottom. The rosy pink blossoms appear in profusion from mid-August through September.

Yesterday-Today-and-Tomorrow

"What's in a name? That which we call a rose by any other name would smell as sweet," said Juliet to Romeo. But somehow the line doesn't ring quite as true when confronted with the appellation of "yesterday-today-and-tomorrow." For such is the descriptive common name of a number of species in the *Brunfelsia* genus, flowers so called because they begin their bloom by appearing in colors of a deep purple that slowly fade over a period of days to pale blue and finally to white.

Brunfelsia was named in honor of Otto Brunfels (1489–1534), a gentleman who began his career as a Carthusian monk, became a Lutheran convert, and finally a physician. He is remembered today for his book *Herbarum Vivae Eicones*, published from 1530 to 1536, one of the first great herbals and an important step in the history of botanical illustration.

The flowers appear from January to April—frequently throughout the year—and are sweetly scented, funnel-shaped with a long tube and a flat, five-lobed lip, and usually open in one color but slowly change with age. Other common names are morning-noon-and-night, yesterday-and-today, and Paraguay jasmine.

They are good candidates for a self-watering pot, since the soil must be kept evenly moist at all times. A good mix is one-third each of potting soil, peat moss, and composted manure. Repotting should be accomplished after the plants cease blooming. Since they are jungle denizens, they appreciate high humidity, and frequent

Yesterday-Today-and-Tomorrow ▶
Brunfelsia pilosa

misting is helpful to their health. Sunlight is necessary most of the year except the hot sun of July and August in a typical southern window.

Over time the plants can become very shrubby and large, flowering profusely, so a good idea is to prune them back before the new growth appears, leading to more compact specimens.

Propagation is by rooted cuttings in heated sand.

Three plants are usually offered: *Brunfelsia australis* bears flowers 1½ inches wide, and *B. pilosa*, from Brazil, has flowers 1¾ inches wide; both change color from purple to white. *B. jamaicensis* comes from the Blue Mountains of Jamaica and has fragrant white to cream-colored flowers that bloom throughout the summer.

The Tree Tomato

The tree tomato has the same kind of questionable cachet as many others that appear on the pages of the *National Enquirer* or like tabloids found in the lanes of the local supermarket. You know the kind I mean—papers that feature headlines like "Grandmother Lives in Basement for Three Weeks on Tiny Fungus!" or "Gardener Grows Potatoes and Tomatoes on the Same Plant!" or "I Was an Earwig for the FBI!" For the tree tomato has often appeared in advertising that never shows a photograph of the plant but only a rather crudely colored drawing of a giant tree festooned with bright red fruit that completely dwarfs the people standing beneath its branches and accompanied with the news that this plant can feed a family of four all winter long with delectable harvests.

Cyphomandra betacea, the tree tomato (*Cyphomandra* is from the Greek for humped man and refers to the shape of the anthers),

belongs to the same family as the garden-variety tomato and the potato. It's a soft-wooded bush that grows to a height of ten to twelve feet in the wild but is considerably smaller in the confines of the home. A fast-growing plant, it's been cultivated for centuries in Central and South America for the edible fruit, but outside of botanical gardens and a few knowledgeable growers in this country, cyphomandras are relatively unknown. It was introduced to the world by James Tweedie (1775–1862), a botanist who trekked the Argentine up to Peru and discovered, in addition to the tree tomato, pampas grass (*Cortaderia Selloana*) and the original ancestor of the bedding petunia, *Petunia violacea*.

Start your plant from seed, or purchase a small specimen from a plant supplier. The plants need a good soil, well laced with organic matter or composted manure, and should be repotted annually until they are at home in a large pot or wooden tub. I use one-third each of potting soil, peat moss, and composted manure, and I fertilize over the summer months every three weeks. If your plant gets too rangy, prune it in April or May.

The fragrant flowers are purple and green, appearing in the spring, although in the right conditions, this plant will flower most of the year. Flowers are followed by orange-red egg-shaped fruits, about three inches long, rich in pectin, with light orange pulp and black seeds. Until mature they taste decidedly mawkish, and ripe fruit—though it can be eaten raw—is best used in jams and preserves or for stewing.

Water well most of the year, holding back only in the midwinter months when light levels are low. Give tree tomatoes plenty of sunlight, and keep temperatures above 50°F—although plants will survive an occasional dip to just above freezing without enjoying it.

Tree Tomato
Cyphomandra betacea

Plants do better in low-humidity situations, so watch out for spider mites, as they find the leaves a delightful place to dine.

The Fig Tree

The fig has a long and colorful history. "And they sewed fig leaves together, and made themselves aprons," comes from the Bible. The Greek poet Menander (342–292 B.C.) remarked, "I call a fig a fig, a spade a spade." (Some years later John Taylor [1580–1653], often called the Water Poet, wrote, "I think it good plain English, without fraud, To call a spade a spade, a bawd a bawd.") And finally John Heywood (1497–1580), the English dramatist, said the following:

Let the world slide, let the world go;
a fig for care, and a fig for woe!
If I can't pay, why I can owe,
And death makes equal the high and low.

The genus is *Ficus*, the old Latin name for the plant, and that in turn comes from the ancient Hebrew *feg*. The species, *carica*, is named for an ancient city in Asia Minor. The plant is unusual in that the flowers are never seen. They line the inside of the fruit, and in many varieties a tiny *blastophaga* or fig wasp enters a small opening at the base of a burgeoning fruit and pollinates the flowers. *Blastophaga*s cannot live in warm climates, so the cultivars 'Adriatic' and 'Turkey' are used in cooler climates, for they are self-pollinating.

This wonderful tree with its legendary fruit has been in continual cultivation for thousands of years because properly ripened figs are not only sweet and delicious but good for you as well. From USDA Zone 7 and south, the common fig can remain outdoors and weather the winter; during its dormant period, it can even withstand temperatures of 10°F. But remember that when it's sprouting, anything freezing or below can severely damage new growth.

As far north as New York City and, in particular, Brooklyn, fig trees will grow outdoors if provided with adequate winter protection, usually consisting of wrapping the trees in layers of burlap, building little wooden sheds (much as the Japanese wrap palm trees in Tokyo), or by bending the trees down to the ground and then covering them with earth.

Figs also make great pot plants using nine- to twelve-inch pots and planting a soil mix of good potting soil, peat moss, composted manure, and sand, one-quarter each. Repot the fig every fall, removing some of the old soil and adding new, or at least top-dress the existing soil. Once in a pot, it needs plenty of water, but let the soil dry between waterings. Fertilize with plant food every month during active growth. Figs also want as much sun as possible, so if you keep them indoors, give them a sunny window.

Remember to spritz the leaves every day if your plants are kept indoors. Figs tend to harbor red spider mites, and these horrors resent water in any form.

Many gardeners without a greenhouse or sun porch will allow the tree to be exposed to a few early frosts to start dormancy, then put it in a cool basement until spring or bring it into a temperature of 65°F and start growth again.

Look for the cultivar 'Brown Turkey', which is self-fertile and will produce fruit the first year it's planted.

Ripened fruit is soft to the touch. Twist the figs, or cut them off.

The Beautiful Gardenia

A few flakes of light snow are falling on this last night of the year. They will not last, for temperatures are too high and the thin clouds are quickly blowing away. Though it's December, the landscape is still barren, fields and woods of brown, not white. Yet in my study, one small white gardenia has opened, its perfume filling the room with thoughts of tropical nights and gentle trade winds.

The gardenia was a gift from a lady who lived down the road. She had cared for the plant for many years since it began as a small houseplant purchased at a local supermarket. Somebody told her that gardenias needed iron to be healthy, so she stuck a wire clothes hanger in the back of the pot, and whatever the reason, the gardenia quickly grew into a shrub four feet in diameter and four feet high, living in a twelve-inch tub.

The *Gardenia* genus is named for Alexander Garden (1730–1791), a Scottish-American naturalist and physician who settled in South Carolina and amazingly discovered the amphibians known as the Congo snake or Congo eel and the siren or mud eel. Because of his Tory sympathies during the War of Independence, he was named a Fellow of the Royal Society.

Requirements for this particular gardenia, *Gardenia jasminoides* var. *Fortuniana* (a double-flowered form), are not taxing, except for warmth—60°F and up. It will survive 50°F without damage, though its dislike for low temperature is clear, for the plant will slowly drop or yellow its leaves. The best temperatures for optimum growth are 65°–85°F. Amazingly enough, bud growth is initiated by temperatures below 65°F. If you especially want winter flowers, pinch off the developing buds until September.

A good soil mix is one-third each of potting soil, peat moss, and sand, and that soil must always be kept evenly moist, as the thin fibrous roots cannot tolerate too much dryness. Fertilize once a month with an acid-based plant food as long as there is active growth. Gardenias want as much full sun as possible, especially during the winter; if light is poor, the buds will drop.

Cuttings can be struck at any time during the year using half- or fully ripened stems taken with a heel.

The yellow fruit that results from fertilized flowers is said to be eaten in China, but my plant has never produced such fruit.

Gardenia jasminoides or the Cape jasmine is often used in baskets, and as long as light is plentiful, it will produce flowers all year long. *G. Thunbergia*, from South Africa, bears intensely fragrant blossoms set among small, elongated diamond-shaped leaves.

The Shrimp Plant

The shrimp plant is one of those few denizens of the plant world that has a common name of such exactitude that no amount of imagination is needed in order to see that the derivation is right on. The blossoms look exactly like a leaping shrimp or prawn getting ready to fly out from amid the leaves. And there is another truth: it's said to be everblooming, and it is.

The genus is *Justicia*, named in honor of James Justice, a Scottish gardener of the nineteenth century. The common name of the genus is water willow. Older books include it in the genus *Belopherone*, *Calliaspidia*, or *Drejerella* and the species *guttata*, but the correct name is *Justicia Brandegeana*. This is a fairly new plant to commerce, having been introduced to the Europen horticultural world in the 1920s, and to that of England and America in the 1930s.

The "shrimps" are really overlapping bracts of a reddish bronze color, and the true blossoms are two-lipped white flowers that peak out from amid the bracts, each bearing two black stamens that resemble the pop-eyes of a crab, and a long pistil with a bead of nectar at the tip.

Since shrimp plants are originally from Mexico, they prefer a warm spot in full sun, so be sure that surrounding temperatures never fall below 50°F. The best soil mix is one-third each of potting soil, composted manure, and peat moss. Allow the dirt to dry completely before rewatering.

Since shrimp plants are three-foot shrubs in nature, they can become quite large and rangy, so keep them pruned back. They are also effective plants in the garden border, where they can spend the summer producing. Then take cuttings for the winter indoors.

Propagation is by cuttings at any time of the year. Remove the developing flower buds until the proper size is reached.

Two cultivars are available: *Justicia Brandegeana* 'Variegata' has leaves that are peppered with white spots, and 'Yellow Queen' has bracts of bright yellow.

The Colorful Kalanchoes

The generic name for the kalanchoes is *Kalanchoe*, said to be the original Chinese term for the Christmas tree kalanchoe, *K. laciniata* (the species name refers to the cut edge of the leaf), one species of this popular group of succulent plants. There are over 125 other species, mostly from Madagascar but also from tropical and southern Africa, India, China, and on to the Malay Peninsula.

The kalanchoes have been popular houseplants because of their interesting foliage and also for their long-lasting flowers. This group could be a good choice for indoor gardeners interested in forming a collection of plants based on one genus.

The most attractive kalanchoe in my window of plants is the kitchingia or coral bell plant (*Kalanchoe uniflora*), originally from Madagascar. This species name refers to the fact that each stem bears a single flower. And what flowers they are: coral red, puffed-up blossoms that resemble tiny hot-air balloons and cover the plant in spring, lasting for almost a month.

Best in a hanging basket, these plants must have plenty of sunlight and require a soil that provides excellent drainage. A combination of potting soil, peat moss, and sand, one-third each, works extremely well. For planting in an open-weave basket, line the container with sheets of sphagnum moss before adding the soil mix. Allow the mix to dry between waterings, and be sure temperatures stay above 50°F.

Around Christmastime, florists always have pots of the Christmas-kalanchoe or *Kalanchoe Blossfeldiana* (named in honor of Robert Blossfeld, a seed and cactus dealer of Potsdam). Also from Madagascar, this plant and its popular cultivar 'Tom Thumb', will provide flowers from Thanksgiving to May. Although the natural flowering period is January, plants can be growing in all parts of the world and flowered at any time of the year by regulating the day length. Plants with as few as two leaves will flower under short-day conditions. Seeds sown in January (using bottom heat) will bloom for the following Christmas if they are shaded with black cloth or black paper or put into a dark place for about four weeks beginning in September, making sure they receive no more than nine hours of

Shrimp Plant
Justicia Brandegeana ▶

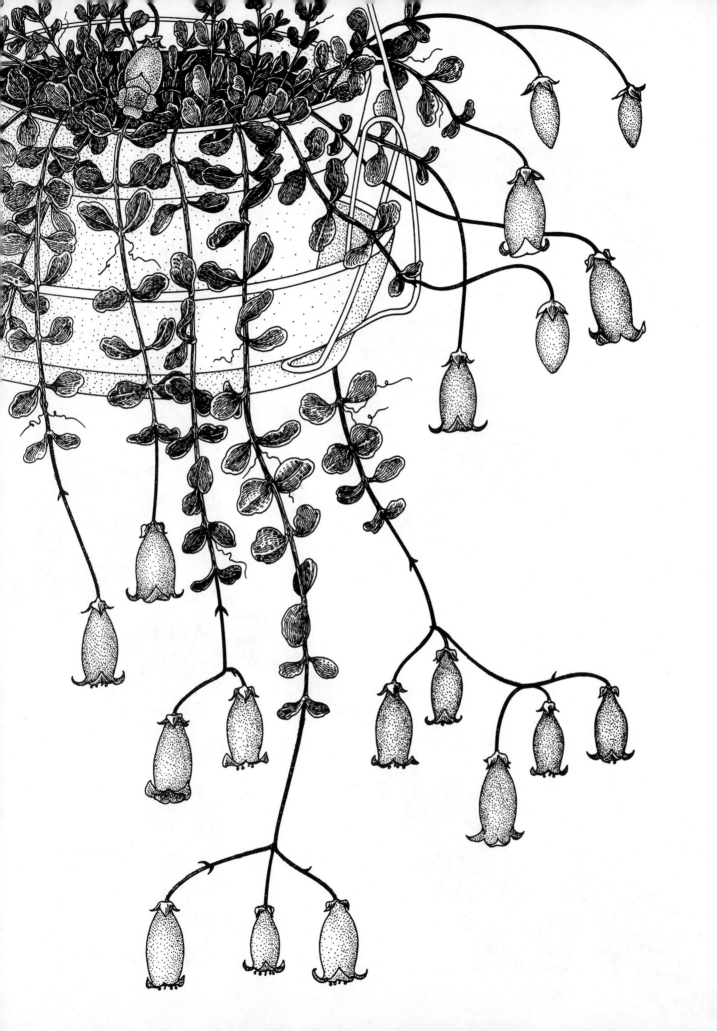

daylight. Cuttings can be taken at any time of the year. Fertilize only during active growth.

The 'Selma Hybrids' are attractive Christmas-kalanchoes, growing easily from seed. They provide a mass of flowers in a color mix of orange, yellow, and red. Like others in the clan, they need full sun and warm temperatures, and the soil should be allowed to dry out between watering.

A number of the kalanchoes are especially interesting because they are viviparous and produce young plants at the tips of their leaves. *Kalanchoe Gastonis-Bonnieri* (named for Gaston Bonnier), or the life plant, is always a conversation piece. These two-foot-high plants have attractive five- to seven-inch succulent, toothed leaves of a pale copper-green dusted with white that produce perfect little plants at the leaf ends, complete with little white roots.

The famous air plant that once was advertised on the back cover of every comic book published in the late thirties and forties is *Kalanchoe pinnata* (*pinnata* means feathery). Other common names include life plant, floppers, Mexican love plant, curtain plant, miracle leaf, good-luck leaf, and, of course, that time-honored term of endearment, the mother-in-law plant.

Nobody really knows the origin of this particular species, since it gives of itself with such abandon. An erect plant up to three feet high, it has leathery leaves of green tinged with red and divided into three to five scalloped leaflets that produce endless clones between the notches. Individual leaves can be removed and pinned to a curtain, and they will continue to produce plantlets until they eventually dry up.

The previously described soil mix is fine for these last two plants. Provide full sun, and never overwater. The plantlets will root with ease.

The Everblooming African Gardenia

According to *Hortus Third*, there are only two species in the genus *Mitriostigma* (*mitra* is Latin for a headband or hat, and refers to the stigma of the flower being caplike), and *M. axillare* is the one slated to be a very important addition to the houseplant fleet.

This plant is a gardenia relative that has everything one could wish for in an indoor plant. The evergreen leaves are glossy green, and from the axils where they meet the stem—the species name refers to this fact—legions of one- to two-inch-long arbutus-shaped white flowers with a touch of pink are in almost continual bloom. The blossoms are fragrant, too.

Originally from Natal, they were for years known as *Gardenia citriodora*, the old species name referring to the fragrance. Eventually the plants can reach a height of five feet.

A good soil mix is one-third each of potting soil, peat moss, and sand. Full sun or light shade are required, and temperatures should stay above 50°F. Keep the soil evenly moist, never letting it dry out. Propagate by cuttings at any time of the year.

The Pregnant Onion

The pregnant onion is another houseplant that always elicits a response from the casual passerby, since when in flower or just resting, its look is decidedly odd. The common names are the false sea onion, the healing onion, or the German onion (Meerzwiebel), but perhaps most to the point is the name of pregnant onion.

The botanical name is *Ornithogalum caudatum*, the genus being Greek for *ornis*, a bird, and *gala*, milk, or bird's milk, and was

Balloons
Kalanchoe uniflora

used by the ancient Greeks as a colloquial expression meaning something wonderful. Well, to each his or her own.

The first common name refers to the plant's resemblance to another plant entirely, the sea squill (*Urginea maritima*); the second to the practice of using the crushed leaves as a cauterizer over cuts and bruises and cooked into a syrup with rock candy for treating the common cold; and the third to the tiny bulbs that appear on the surface of the mother bulb, growing larger until they fall to the earth and become new plants.

Set the parent bulb with most of its girth above a standard soil mix of one-third each potting soil, composted manure, and sharp sand. Soon long, curved, and straplike leaves, sometimes two feet long, will fall over the pot's edge.

If given good light, full sun whenever possible, and temperatures of 50°–65°F, and if you remember to water only after the soil has dried out, a long flower stalk will soon appear—often reaching a length of three feet—carrying 50 to 100 small white flowers with each petal bearing a green median stripe. The flowers will bloom from the bottom over a long period of time, and the stalk tends to bend and twist in many directions.

The pregnant feature of the plant is perhaps its most noticeable trait, as evidenced by the bulbils shown in the drawing. Don't remove them until they are free of the parent bulb's membrane. When placed on warm soil, in good light, the bulbils will soon grow into new plants. After blooming is past, give the mother bulb a short rest by withholding water.

The Charming Oxalis

According to *Hortus Third*, there are over 850 species of *oxalis*, with the greatest number in South Africa and South America. One of the most beautiful wildflowers of a northern forest is the wood sorrel, *Oxalis montana*, and one of the most pernicious weeds, especially to greenhouse owners, is the pesky yellow wood sorrel, *O. stricta*. The latter is a nuisance because the seed pods split open with an explosive charge that sends seeds flying for a great distance.

Oxalis is from a Greek word for sharp, referring to the acid taste of the leaves. The chemical involved is called oxalic acid and is poisonous in large quantities, but the leaves of the European *O. Acetosella* have been used to flavor soups and salads for years.

A number of these plants are suitable for growing as houseplants, but there are two I find especially delightful. One is everblooming, and the other blooms in spring, with the bulbs being dormant in summer.

Oxalis Regnellii originally came from Brazil and south. It has beautiful white flowers and attractive shamrock-type foliage—somewhat square cut, not rounded, and purple underneath—blooming most of the time. I've had a pot in continual flower since the spring of 1986, and it shows no sign of slowing down. The soil mix is one-quarter each of potting soil, peat moss, composted manure, and sand. Temperatures should always be above 50°F, and full to partial sun is necessary for the fullest flowering and best leaf color.

Amazingly enough, *O. Regnellii* will bloom in a north window, and a good gardening friend has had a small plant set in an attractive basket on her kitchen table, five feet away from an east window, that has bloomed for five years.

Oxalis braziliensis blooms in spring over

African Gardenia ▶
Mitriostigma axillare

a period of two months. The flower petals are wine red on the top, about the color of a good burgundy, and paler beneath. By summer the leaves disappear, and the plant goes into dormancy, with growth resuming in the late fall.

The Voodoo Lily

Since the listing of the plant is alphabetically by the genus name, the voodoo lily or *Sauromatum guttatum* will appear before *Serissa foetida*, and it's a shame because, of the two, the voodoo lily has by far the worse odor. The genus comes from the Latin *sauros*, for lizard, and *oura*, tail, and refers to the very long spadix that emerges from the wrinkled spathe. *Guttatum* means spotted. Other common names include the red calla and monarch-of-the-east. The plant comes from Southeast Asia and India, where it is one of only four species. Older books call *S. guttatum* by the species name of *venosum*, meaning prominent veining, but *guttatum* is a better choice.

This plant is rarely pictured in plant catalogs, and when it does appear, the likeness is usually in a little watercolor or a hurried drawing, never by a photograph. To begin with, the blossom when open is not very photogenic because of the inordinate length of the purple spadix—often fourteen inches long. And I wonder, too, if it was pictured, just how many people would buy it. After all, it is decidedly a novelty.

In the spring and shortly after you water the pot that contains the wrinkled, oval-shaped tuber (or tubers), a pale green tip will push up through the dirt. Day by day it will lengthen, until finally the spathe will open to reveal an inner lining of purple spots on a greenish-buff background. Also disclosed will be the lizard's tail, a

dark purple bending wand, its bottom hidden within a part of the spathe that doesn't open and itself sits on a very short, tiny stem, so the blossom is almost level with the soil.

The blossom lasts only a day or two before it deflates and slowly dries up. But now more green tips appear, and soon very large and attractive, tropical-looking leaves appear on spotted stems and will persist until fall. The leaves often reach a height of two feet. The foliage is attractive enough that it could be grown without the added attraction of the bizarre flowers.

If the timing is correct, an unplanted tuber will bloom in spring if it is set on a sunny windowsill. In years past, this was one of the novelties connected with the plant.

Use a soil mix of one-quarter each potting soil, composted manure, peat moss, and sand, and plant two or three tubers two inches deep in a six-inch pot. Keep temperatures above 60°F, and give the plant partial shade, since the noonday sun of July and August is too much for the leaves. Water well when the plant is in active growth, and fertilize once a month until the leaves die back and yellow. Then store the pot in a cool, dark place until the following spring.

The Serissa

According to the *RHS Dictionary of Gardening*, there is only one member found in the genus *Serissa*, and that is the species *foetida*, originally from Southeast Asia and introduced to the horticultural world in 1787. *Hortus Third* reports one species, perhaps three, but only mentions *S. foetida*. *Serissa* is the old Indian name for the plant, and you know what *foetida* means.

I think we have another case of a plant

◀ Pregnant Onion
Ornithogalum caudatum

(following page)
Oxalis
Oxalis braziliensis ▶

getting a bad name from an overstatement on what truly represents a bad smell. Both tomes say the bark is fetid when bruised, and *Hortus* claims the leaves, too, have an odor that leaves much to be desired.

Now, I know plants that have a bad smell. When in bloom, the Devil's-tongue (*Amorphophallus Rivieri*) has an odor so powerfully putrid that people put handkerchiefs over their noses and run, not walk, from a room where the blossom is open to the air. And a number of the larger species of the stapelias (which see) smell like a combination of dirty sneakers mixed with three-day-old hamburger left out in July. The aroma from the seeds of the female ginkgo tree is that of rancid butter and should never be planted close to any segment of refined society. But pity the poor serissa. At worst the smell is slightly foxy, and at best it isn't there at all.

I first saw the plant in the temperate greenhouse of the Brooklyn Botanic Garden. It was an attractive bush about two feet high, covered with tiny, shiny green leaves, each edged with a thin line of creamy white and boasting dozens of single half-inch long pink flowers. The name was *Serissa foetida* 'Variegata', also called the yellow-rim serissa, because the variegations have a slight yellow tone when new.

They are excellent plants for dish gardens and indoor bonsai, as they respond well to pruning and shaping.

A good soil mix is one-third each potting soil, peat moss, and sand. Serissa likes a place in partial sun with evenly moist soil. Fertilize every few months when the plants are in active growth.

There are a number of cultivars. *Serissa foetida* 'Flora Plena' is called the snow rose and bears double white flowers that resemble tiny roses; *S. foetida* 'Kyoto' is said to be excellent for topiary and bears single white flowers; *S. foetida* 'Mt. Fuji' has variegated foliage, with each leaf edged

with bands of pure white; and *S. foetida* 'Sapporo' is a fastigiate form—its branches turn upward and lie close to the main stem—with tiny white flowers and dense foliage.

The Sophisticated Calla Lilies

Back in the Manhattan of the 1930s, when displaced members of the middle class tried to earn a living by selling apples on the corner of Seventh Avenue and Forty-Second Street, the movies presented a different world, a world of sophistication and pizazz, a world of martinis in crystal glasses, evening dresses topped with ostrich feathers, and elegant tables for dining set upon black marble floors, all in front of floor-to-ceiling windows that looked out upon the city bathed in a combination of searchlights and theater lights, but definitely with a feeling of fairy lights. And in the center of every table in a tall bud vase was one calla lily, its organic shape echoed in wall standards of white frosted glass and plaster anaglyphs high in the ceilings. Fred and Ginger danced, and the calla was the flower of the decade—at least on the silver screen.

It's an African plant of the genus *Zantedeschia*, named in honor of Francesco Zantedeschi (1773–1846), an Italian physician and botanist. Originally it belonged to the genus *Calla* (from the Greek *kallos*, for beauty), but this name was given to the water arum or *Calla palustris* (the species is a Latin term for marsh-loving), and the calla had to find a new nomenclature, so a French botanist, L. C. Richard (1754–1821), was summoned, but he eventually lost out to Francesco. The species is *aethiopica*, named for the peoples of northeast Africa, and the plant was

introduced into Europe in 1687.

Up until last year, I grew calla lilies the time-honored way: in a pot until late summer, when the foliage was allowed to die down and yellow, then water was withheld and the rhizomes allowed to rest until being repotted in spring.

Then I saw a reference by William Robinson in *The English Flower Garden* that callas were basically aquatic evergreen plants that grew freely in the ditches and swamps of South Africa. So I planted the rhizomes in the fall of 1988 in an eight-inch plastic pot using a soil mix of one-quarter each potting soil, peat moss, composted manure, and sand. First I watered well, then placed the pot in a waterproof crock and filled that with water up to the level of the soil. The temperature never fell below 55°F, and the plants receive full sun. In addition, callas are heavy feeders, so I fertilize every month while in active growth. If you are repotting them, add fresh manure each time.

Within a few weeks, the first green leaves pushed up, and they soon grew into handsome spear-shaped, glossy green leaves between two and three feet high. Then the first flowers appeared in January. And what flowers they were: a pure white (calla haters always say "dead white") folded spathe that surrounds a bright yellow spadix and soon gives off a lovely sweet fragrance that delights a winter's day.

The tiny true flowers surround the spadix, with the males on the upper part of the column and the females below. If left alone, they will set seed.

In about two months the flowers stopped, and I cut them off, but new leaves continued to appear. Then in April, the growth stopped, and the leaves yellowed and fell away. I continued to water but left the pot alone until mid-May, when I set it out in the garden pond. In the heat of June and July, new leaves appeared, and the cycle began again.

There are probably a number of combinations that can be used to grow this lovely plant, so experimentation is in order. They are winter-hardy in USDA Zone 8, so they could be lovely in an outdoor garden where winters are mild.

Watch out for spider mites. They have a predilection for the taste of calla leaves.

Calla Lily
Zantedeschia aethiopica ▶

PART TWO

PLANTS FOR FOLIAGE

While flowers have always captured the public's imagination, there is much to be said for a garden composed of foliage. Since few plants bloom year-round, the leaves become very important to the decorating scheme created for an indoor garden. The following plants are all elegant in leaf.

The Chinese Evergreens

The botanical name for the Chinese evergreen is *Aglaonema* from *aglaos*, meaning bright, and *nema*, for thread, perhaps referring to the shining stamens of the flower. I asked a number of houseplant experts if anyone knew the derivation of the name, but nobody had a clue.

The common name of Chinese evergreen originated with *Aglaonema modestum*. According to the *Aglaonema Growers Notebook* (now out of print but well worth the search), this particular plant has been in continual cultivation by the Chinese for centuries and is found in the northern part of Thailand, in adjoining Laos, and in areas of China and North Vietnam. Almost all the people of Asia own at least one *A. modestum* because the plant is thought to bring good luck, and in the Philippines this particular Chinese evergreen is known as *la suerte*, again for good luck.

The author of the *Growers Notebook*, Roy N. Jervis, treats nineteen species and reminds us that only twelve are in general cultivation, and although there are less than twenty-four botanically valid species, the varieties, forms, and cultivars in use today total more then one hundred names.

Aglaonemas belong to the Araceae or Arum family and include herbs, climbers, and a few shrubs, all with large simple or compound leaves and a flower that—like the calla lily and the flamingo flower—consists of a spathe that surrounds a spadix.

Another word applied to these plants is *tough*. They succeed in very dim light—surviving with as little as ten to fifteen footcandles (see Introduction) but preferring at least the light from a north window for a few days every month or additional illumination from artificial lighting.

Potting soil should be well drained and include peat moss. A good mix here is one-third each of soil, peat moss, and sand. Keep the mix evenly moist; Chinese evergreens respond well to self-watering pots.

They will also grow quite well in pure water. Any vessel that will hold water will serve—except for copper, brass, or lead. Take the plant out of the pot, remove the excess earth, then carefully wash the roots in clear, tepid water. Add a few small pieces of charcoal in the bottom of the container, then add the plant and enough water to cover the roots and part of the stem. Never let any leaves remain under the water surface, as they will rot. Don't forget the charcoal: it is important because it will keep the water clean. As the water evaporates, replace it with fresh water. And don't use chlorinated water. If that's all you have, run a sinkful of water and let it sit for thirty-six hours. Also, do not use water softened by a home appliance. Plants do not like the chemicals involved.

Temperature can be a problem, since these plants must be kept warm, especially when grown in water. The roots are especially sensitive to cold. During the day, 75°–85°F is ideal, with a drop of ten degrees at night.

GROWING PLANTS FROM SEED

To grow Chinese evergreens from seed, clean the red pulp off of the outside of a fruit to reveal a large, peanut-sized green seed. Place the seed on a bed of moist sphagnum moss or any clean soil. Keep the temperatures above 65°F, and don't cover the seed, as it needs light for germination, a process that averages about three weeks.

HYBRIDIZING CHINESE EVERGREENS

To hybridize, take the pollen from a male

Clown Fig
Ficus aspera; Spider Plant
Chlorophytum comosum variegatum; Screw Pine ▶
Pandanus Veitchii; Cast-Iron Plant
Aspidistra elatior 'Variegata'

flower of one species or cultivar and collect it in a small piece of aluminum foil. Then tap some of this pollen on the opening female flowers of another plant. To prevent self-fertilization in nature, a plant's flowers do not bloom at the same time; the females open first, and the males follow.

The Biggest Aspidistra in the World

During the Second World War, the English music hall singer and comedian Gracie Fields kept the home fires burning bright with her boisterous rendition of "It Was the Biggest Aspidistra in the World," a song urging Britons to rally round the things that made England great, including more homes and parlors with more "blooming aspidistras" than any other country in the world.

In 1823 John Damper Parks sailed on the *Lowther Castle* from London to China and brought back, among roses, chrysanthemums, and camellias, the very first aspidistra, a plant that by 1840 suited the burgeoning Victorian generation to a capital T. Amazingly impervious to bad air, bad light, bad smoke, and thick dust, it was a perfect plant to set among Turkish cushions in dark and dreary cozy corners. In fact, it soon gained the popular name of the cannon-ball plant, or in some circles the cast-iron plant thanks to its ability to withstand all sorts of ill treatment.

The genus is *Aspidistra* from the Greek for a small, round shield, referring to the shape of the flower's stigma. The species was first termed *lurida* and came from the so-called lurid purple flowers that occasionally appear at ground level, but the species name used today is *elatior*, meaning taller, having to do with the size of the leaf.

The flowers are more interesting than beautiful, consisting of six to eight brownish-purple sections, not really petals, that open to reveal a disk with eight stamens and that in nature are fertilized by wandering slugs.

The leaves are a leathery, dark green, up to 2½ feet long. Use a potting mix of one-third each potting soil, peat moss, and sand, and try to keep it evenly moist, although the plant will live up to its common names and go for weeks without water. Temperatures should always be above 50°F. Aspidistras do not take kindly to full sun, so give them a spot in partial shade, especially during the hot summer months.

There is a very attractive variegated form known as 'Variegata', which has leaves patterned with alternating white strips on a green background. A dwarf variety called 'Milky Way' has leaves beautifully shaded with ivory spots.

If you are in a hurry to develop a large plant with a pot full of leaves, buy a number of smaller plants, and bunch them together.

The Ponytail Palm

The ponytail palms are on rare occasions found in the genus *Nolina*, botanical nomenclature that is easy to explain, since this appellation is in honor of P. C. Nolin, a Frenchman who wrote on agriculture in the Paris of 1755. Unfortunately most authorities include this plant in the genus *Beaucarnea*, which means beautiful flesh-colored something, and since the flowers are usually white, I have been unable to find the true meaning. The species found in cultivation is *recurvata*, and that's easy to understand, since the leaves cascade to the floor in gentle curves that often curve again, making it a most attractive plant to have. This is one of those plants that make

Ponytail Palm ▶
Beaucarnea recurvata

an architectural statement, especially in a modern home or apartment with lots of glass, chrome, and white walls or in a place with the decor found in the American Southwest.

In the wilds of southern Texas and Mexico, this treelike plant can reach a height of thirty feet, but in the usual home surroundings—where the owner can take advantage of its ability to survive in a small pot and withstand forgetful waterings—the height rarely tops six feet. The leaves are flat, three-quarters of an inch wide, and often reach a length of five feet. A well-grown ponytail palm has a Rapunzel-like quality.

The other common name is elephant-foot tree and refers to the ponderous shape of the trunk's base, a shape that resembles a balloon made of rigid bark. This swelling soaks up water like a sponge and allows the plant to store water—in a large ponytail—for up to a year. While a potted specimen will not put up with that intensity of neglect, it will survive for months without water if the basal swelling exceeds four or five inches.

In fact, there are two approaches to care. The first is to provide the ponytail with an evenly moist soil and a spot with partial shade, and the second is to keep the soil on the dry side and set the plant in a sunny spot. Just remember that a well-watered plant will grow twice as fast.

While ponytails can withstand temperatures in the high forties, they prefer temperatures of 55°–70°F. A good soil mix consists of one-quarter each potting soil, peat moss, composted manure, and sand. Fertilize only once or twice a year.

The expanding trunks will adjust to crowded conditions, but eventually the plants have to be moved to a larger pot. Perform this operation in early spring before the new leaves appear.

Many ponytails in cultivation have leaves about three feet long and belong to the variety *intermedia*.

The Peacock and Prayer Plants

The peacock plants of the genus *Calathea* and the prayer plants of the genus *Maranta* both belong to the Maranta family. Although the flowers are pretty, they are small and completely overshadowed by the exceptionally beautiful leaves, which appear in such luxurious colors and color combinations that they surely must rival those found in Joseph's coat. Both are native to tropical America.

THE PEACOCK PLANTS

Calathea is supposedly derived from the first botanical description, when an unknown botanist saw the leaves of *C. lutea* used in basket making (the leaves also produce a wax similar to carnauba), hence the Greek word *calathos*, meaning basket. The common name of peacock plant is obvious upon seeing this plant.

My favorite is *Calathea Makoyana*, a species that is originally from Brazil and bears large oval leaves—often a foot long—that are patterned on both sides: the top with olive green lines and ovals over a field of pale yellow-green, while underneath the pattern is repeated in a rich purple-red.

But running a close second is *Calathea Warscewiczii*, a species from Costa Rica that bears very dark green leaves feathered with paler green markings on either side of the midrib and purple underneath. The plant is named in honor of a Polish botanist, Joseph Warscewicz (1812–1866).

At least twelve different species and cultivars are available, including a number of dwarf plants if space is limited.

Prayer and Peacock Plants
◀ *Calathea Makoyana* and *Maranta leuconeura* var. *Kerchoviana*

Peacock plants like a humid atmosphere much as is found in their jungle homes. Keep the soil evenly moist—these plants do well in self-watering pots—and use a mix of one-fifth each potting soil, composted manure, sand, peat moss, and perlite or vermiculite. Prepared African violet soil is excellent. Full sun must be avoided, as the leaves will burn. Keep the plants in filtered sun or strong artificial light. Fertilize once a month during active growth, and never feed plants until they have settled in. Don't let temperatures fall below 60°F.

These plants stop growing from the end of December until February, so watering should be cut back at that time. If they are in a self-watering pot, let the reservoir dry out at that time, and water only when the soil becomes dry. Plants should be divided in early spring before new growth occurs.

THE PRAYER PLANTS

The prayer plants belong to the genus Maranta and were named in honor of Bartolomea Maranti, a Venetian botanist who flourished in the mid-1500s. They are aptly named, because the foliage patterns strongly suggest those found in Venetian glass. The word *prayer* refers to the plant's habit of curling up its leaves at night and unfurling them in the morning.

Three varieties of *Maranta leuconeura* (the species name refers to light veining or pattern of nerves) are commonly found in cultivation. Var. *erythroneura* (*erythro* is a fifty-dollar word for red) bears leaves up to five inches long that exhibit a herringbone design of carmine veining that overlays a background of a velvety olive green, and is the most beautiful of the three. Var. *Kerchoviana* (named for Oswald Charles Eugène Kerchove de Denterghem [1844–1906]) has dark brown and dark green splotches on a light green background. And var. *leuconeura* has silvery gray feathering on a black-green background.

The Fancy Caladiums

For most of the year, the majority of the plants in this book produce either attractive foliage, flowers, or both. Caladiums are an exception: their flowers are interesting rather than beautiful, and they spend part of the year in complete dormancy without a sign of their presence, but the leaves are so spectacular they are worth a major effort to grow them in the window. There are about fifteen species in the genus *Caladium* (named for the Malay word *kalady*), most having beautifully marked leaves and originally hailing from South America.

Their one weakness is sensitivity to cold. Never start them indoors unless the tubers can be kept warm, and never plant the tubers outside until night temperatures go no lower than 55°–60°F and the soil is very warm. Yet when they leaf out, keep those leaves out of direct sunlight during the hot summer months, or the foliage will be scorched and burned.

Caladium bicolor is usually called angel-wings, sometimes mother-in-law plant (why, I cannot fathom), and in tropical countries the heart-of-Jesus. This species is probably the chief parent behind today's many exotic cultivars. It is also an important tropical food crop; the gingerlike roots are boiled and eaten under the name of cocoa roots. In addition, a purgative medicine is extracted from fresh rhizomes.

The original plant grows about thirty inches high and bears arrow-shaped leaves—or elongated hearts—fourteen inches long by ten inches wide. The leaves are red with a broad red border on purple stems.

Caladium Hybrids ▶
Caladium ✕ *hortulanum*

From this humble beginning hundreds of cultivars have been created. Tubers can be ordered from major nurseries and come in a bewildering variety of colors.

Caladiums arrived in the Europe of the 1850s, and the first cultivar was 'Chantinii' introduced in 1857 and named for a French nursery. Basically it resembles the original plant, but the leaves are flecked with various bits of white. This was followed by 'Splendens', which arrived from South America in 1773 and bears red-purple veins on a green background.

Among the newest are the following choices, each reaching a height of two feet: 'Carolyn Wharton' with large, bright pink leaves, rose veins, and the entire leaf surface flecked with green; 'White Christmas', which has white leaves with green veins; and 'Red Flash', which produces leaves with bright red centers and deep ribs surrounded with splashes of pink.

There are shorter varieties, too, growing about eighteen inches high. These include 'Rose Bud', with dark green borders that blend into white, then turn to a rose-pink around the veins, and 'Frieda Hemple', which bears solid red leaves bordered with green.

And finally a new miniature has arrived on the scene, growing about eight inches tall, which can be used as a border for the larger types. It's called 'Little Miss Muffet' and has lime green leaves marked with splotches of wine red.

Propagation is by little tubers that grow around the edge of mature tubers and by homegrown seed (although seedlings usually vary greatly).

Plant the dormant tubers just below the soil surface—knobby side up—in six-inch pots, and keep them at 70°F until the leaves appear. Use a potting mix of one-third each potting soil, composted manure, and sand. Water well whenever the soil is dry, and fertilize once a month while the plants are in active growth.

During periods of hot weather, syringe the leaves with warm water, and turn the pots every day to keep the leaves from growing in one direction.

In the fall withhold water, and store the pots in a warm spot—never below 60°F—until the following spring. Then replace the first inch of soil with fresh, bring into heat, and the tubers will grow again. Tubers can also be removed from the pots and stored in a bed of sphagnum or peat moss.

Often when the tubers are receptive to their environment, they will bloom. The flowers have a unisexual spadix surrounded by a spathe, as they are members of the same family as flamingo flowers and jack-in-the-pulpit.

Watch out for spider mites!

Beautiful Dizzy

Recently a friend asked about the care and nurture of a fairly popular houseplant known as the false aralia, spider aralia, threadleaf, splitleaf maple, or, by those in the know, dizzy. The botanical name is *Dizygotheca elegantissima*, the genus meaning a two-yoke case because the anthers have double the usual number of cells. The species name is obvious because it is such an elegant and beautiful plant.

Originally discovered in the New Hebrides Islands (now known as Vanuatu) about 1870, this shrub will eventually grow into a small tree of about twenty-five feet tall, but generally not in the average home.

Confusion began some years ago over the various stages of the life of dizzy. When the plant is young and shrubby, its leaves are compound and sit on long, dark green-and-white mottled stems, the seven to ten arching leaflets toothed and graceful.

At maturity, the leaf character changes: leaflets become lance-shaped and generally broader, and the toothed edge becomes lobed. For a while botanists puzzled over the true identity of the plant, and it was placed in the *Aralia* genus (as were a number of other genera). It is still offered occasionally as *Aralia laciniata*.

The leathery leaves appear to be a copper color until they mature and become a deep green that almost seems black.

Plants do best in filtered sun or bright indirect light in temperatures always above 60°F. Keep the soil evenly moist because these plants originally come from a jungle environment. Use a soil mix of one-third each potting soil, peat moss, and sand, and fertilize every month during the spring and summer. Repot plants in early spring before new growth commences. Propagation is by stem cuttings.

Two other species are sometimes offered for sale. *Dizygotheca Kerchoveana* has a very pale midrib, and *D. Veitchii* has leaves that are green on top and coppery red beneath. This last plant was found growing on New Caledonia in 1865 by John Gould Veitch, who was unable to explore many of the islands in the South Pacific because of the hostility of the inhabitants. At one point a local chief was held on board Veitch's ship as a hostage to guarantee Veitch's safety while he roamed swamps up to his armpits, looking for new species.

There is a new cultivar called 'Pink Rim'. Its leaflets are margined in soft pink when young.

The Japanese Medlar or Loquat

A friend of mine who travels yearly to Florida brought back some loquat seeds for me in the spring of 1988 and assured me that, as a container plant for the home, the loquat would surprise me with its reasonably quick growth and the attractiveness of its leaves.

I planted the seeds in late spring, using three-inch clay pots and a soil mix of potting soil, peat, and sand, one-third each, and placed the pots on a heating cable. By the time autumn came around, there were three leaves on each seedling.

The leaves themselves are rather strange, being gray-green, soft, and covered with a woolly down both top and bottom. As the leaves mature, the down on the tops of the leaves can be rubbed off—rather like lint—revealing a dark green, leathery surface. The nether down will stay.

By the time the tree had reached a height of eight inches, it possessed ten leaves, the last three being one foot long. By the summer of 1989, the loquat had grown to fourteen inches, had eighteen leaves, and continued to grow.

The botanical name is *Eriobotrya japonica*. *Erion* is the Greek for wool, and *botrys* for cluster, referring to the 1½-inch-long fruit that is covered with a soft, downy skin.

The trees have been cultivated in China and Japan for centuries. Loquats were introduced into Britain in 1787, where they were popular in the glasshouses of the large and stately homes and gardens. Common names include Japanese medlar tree, Japanese plum, and Chinese loquat.

When prepared for cold weather, a tree will survive temperatures of 15°F, but the new shoots will be killed by just a few degrees below freezing. So in most of the country the loquat is best used as a container plant and provided with temperatures of 50°–65°F, a sunny window, and lime-free soil kept evenly moist at all times. This final requirement makes the loquat a good choice for a self-watering

pot, but even then the soil should be loose. The mix I used for the seedlings is fine for the maturing tree.

In the spring, when the loquat reaches a height of 2–2½ feet, it should be pruned so the two or three main branches will develop.

The flowers are white and fragrant, each about a half-inch wide and borne in woolly panicles up to eight inches long. They are said to be most profuse after a long, hot summer.

Most references say that seed-grown trees take many years to reach the state of flowering and I've found that to be true. But meantime, the loquat is well worth growing for its noble and decorative foliage and for the form of the tree.

The Clown Fig

According to *Hortus Third*, the fig family includes food; fodder; natural rubber; bark cloth; the banyan tree, which sends down aerial roots forming trunks to support the canopy, thus allowing the tree to cover several acres; the strangler figs, which begin as plants that live in the open air, then strangle their host and eventually become self-supporting trees; and the host plants for the lac insect, which secretes a resinous substance that, when melted, becomes shellac.

A number of figs make great plants for the window garden including the edible fig (which see), the rubber plant, the weeping fig (one of the most common container plants in today's smart, new office buildings), and the clown fig.

The clown fig is an apt name for a plant that has a distinct feel of delight. From its winsome variegations to its striped fruit, this is a fig to lift the spirits. The botanical name is *Ficus aspera*, with *Ficus*

being the old Latin name for this genus and *aspera* being either an old Latin word for rough (referring to the roughness of the upper leaf) or an old Greek word for white (literally the whiteness of silver coins).

Often called *Ficus Parcellii* in older reference books, the clown fig is a small shrub or a small tree with eight-inch leaves that are dotted and splashed with ivory dabs against a light green background. The figlike fruits are about one inch in diameter and are striped with green, white, and pink.

Of the plants described in this book, the clown fig is not one of the easiest to cultivate, for it will drop its leaves in response to a chill, and it's very prone to spider mites. So if you would rather grow an old war-horse, find a rubber plant, but if you are willing to give just a bit of extra effort, read on, and adopt a clown fig.

Use a soil mix of one-quarter each potting soil, peat moss, composted manure, and sand. Give the plant a spot in partial sun, and be sure to keep it warm in winter, never letting the temperature fall below 60°F. Water well, and then let the soil dry before watering again. Propagate by cuttings.

As to spider mites, they truly love the leaves of the clown fig, so the price of a healthy plant is eternal vigilance, especially during the summer months. Check the underleaves of your plants at least once a week. If these horrors do appear, immediately treat with insecticidal soap, or wash the leaves in the bathtub or sink, using Ivory soap or its equivalent.

The Velvet Plant

The look of a velvet plant presages something out of the ordinary, for it could easily be the favorite houseplant of the

Loquat
Eriobotrya japonica

Wicked Queen in Snow White or perhaps be found growing in the musty basement where the Spider Woman outwitted Sherlock Holmes. The genus is *Gynura* and comes from the Greek *gyne*, for female, and *oura*, tail, and refers to the long and rough stigma in the flower. The name is not, in fact, a very romantic one for a plant with the look of this.

The green leaves and stems are soft to the touch, since they are completely covered with a purple plush, much like the velour that was once used to cover seats in railroad cars. If you look directly down on a leaf, it is green stippled with purple, but when looked at slightly askew, the hairs are all in evidence.

The flowers are orange and really pop when seen against the plushy background of the leaves. They are immediately recognized as placing the plants in the daisy family, but resemblance to most of the daisies ends with floral construction, because they smell exactly like the contents of a dust bag in an old vacuum cleaner.

Two species are generally found in cultivation. *Gynura aurantiaca* is known as the royal velvet plant (the species name means yellow-orange and refers to the flower). Originally from Java, this is the plant usually offered by nurseries.

Gynura sarmentosa (with *sarmentosa* meaning long runners) is in reality a cultivar of *G. aurantiaca* and is properly known as 'Purple Passion'. This particular variety has narrower leaves, and the stems clamber about and are quite effective when seen edging over the lip of a hanging basket. There is another cultivar in this species called 'Aurea-Variegata', which consists of creamy yellow splashes on the purple background and should be eschewed, as it resembles nothing more than a purple sweatshirt that has been sprayed with liquid bleach, with a most unappetizing result.

Gynura bicolor hails from the Moluccas, the same islands that gave birth to the green-blossomed annual flower bells-of-Ireland, leading one to think that a typical pastoral scene hereabouts is garish to say the least. The leaves are purplish-green above and purple beneath.

Velvet plants are easy to grow. The best soil mix is one-quarter each of potting soil, peat moss, composted manure, and sand. Keep temperatures above 60°F, and give these plants a spot in partial shade, although *Gynura bicolor* will take more sun. All the varieties like a soil that is evenly moist. Fertilize every month or so when in active growth. Propagation is by cuttings.

The Leopard Plant

Ligularias are plants from Europe and Asia that belong to the daisy family. Most of them are excellent outdoor perennials for the flower garden, but one, *Ligularia tussilaginea*, comes from Japan and, being less hardy than most of the others, makes an acceptable and attractive houseplant species. In areas colder than USDA Zone 7, it usually does not survive.

Because this plant resembles coltsfoot, *Tussilago farfara*—a perennial herb whose roots are used to prepare a tonic for the relief of coughing—its species name came to be *tussis*, itself an old Latin word for cough. Older catalogs call it *Farfugium grande* and *Senecio Kaempferi*.

Ligularia comes from the Latin *ligula*, which means little tongue and refers to the tonguelike shape of the large petal on each of the ray flowers surrounding the central "eye" of the simpler disk flowers. When we as children played "She (or he) loves me, she (he) loves me not," we tossed away one ray flower of the typical field daisy for each pronouncement and finally were left holding the button of yellow disk flowers.

Royal Velvet Plant
Gynura aurantiaca ▶

To make things more interesting, the common *Ligularia tussilaginea* is never cultivated, but three cultivars are. The first, and in my mind the most attractive, is the leopard plant, *L. tussilaginea* 'Aureo-maculata', a cultivar with kidney-shaped leaves, scalloped on the edge, and each leaf covered with round yellow spots of various sizes. The daisylike flowers are little, light yellow, and completely unimportant when compared to the lovely leaves. 'Argentea' has leaves edged in white, and in strong light the young leaves have a pink cast. 'Crispata', or the parsley ligularia, has green leaves that are ruffled and crisped along the edge.

Since these plants are happy outdoors in much of the temperate zone, they do not like too much heat, so temperatures should never go above 75°F in the summer and 60°F during the winter months. They all like to be kept evenly moist, and a good soil mix is one-quarter each potting soil, peat moss, composted manure, and sand. Keep these plants in partial shade, as too much sun can burn the leaves. Fertilize only while the plant is in active growth, and then only every other month. Propagation is by division in the early spring.

The Mango

Almost everyone has grown an avocado in his or her day, but have you ever thought of starting a mango tree? With today's supersonic delivery systems, fresh mangoes are often found at the local supermarket, right between the pomegranates and the kumquats—and you can always ask someone from Florida to send a pit up north.

Mangifera indica (from *mango*, the Hindu name for the fruit and *fero*, to bear) is believed to have first appeared somewhere in eastern Asia, where it's been under cultivation for over four thousand years. Between A.D. 632 and A.D. 640, a Chinese traveler, Hwen T'sang, brought the tree to the outside world; and by the 1700s, mangoes were grown under glass by most of the nobility of Europe. The following passage is taken from an 1850 issue of *Curtis's Botanical Magazine*:

The mango is recorded as having been grown in the hot-houses of this country at least 160 years ago but it is only within the last 20 years that it has come to the notice as a fruit capable of being brought to perfection in England. The first and we believe the most successful attempt was made by the Earl of Powis in his garden at Walcot where he had a lofty hot-house 400 feet long and between 30 and 40 feet wide constructed for the cultivation of the mango.

Obviously our local mangoes—at least in the colder areas of the country—will not be grown for the fruit but merely as a fascinating houseplant. The seeds (or pits) are rather perishable and will not tolerate much drying. Seeds kept at temperatures lower than 50°F do not germinate at all well, so don't attempt it if the fruit has been refrigerated for a long period of time.

Wash the pit well of pulp, and plant it not more than one-inch deep in sterile potting soil or any commercial growing mix. Put the pit in a warm place (the warmer the better), trying to maintain at least 70°F. My first plant germinated in the heat of a compost heap, where temperatures in excess of 120°F are common, during the month of October. I might add that the first appearance of the sprout was some surprise.

When seedlings are six inches tall, transplant to a six-inch pot, using a soil mix of good potting soil, composted manure, and clean sand, one-third each.

Leopard Plant
Ligularia tussilaginea 'Aureo-maculata' ▶

During the summer months, provide plenty of water. From September to March, let the soil dry out between waterings. In about three years from the time of germination, you can force the tree to blossom by following this watering schedule. The key to flowering is a dry atmosphere with plenty of sunlight. Fertilize every month during the summer months.

Provide as much sun as possible, and always keep the mango warm, with temperatures above 50°F.

As the tree grows, repot it in larger containers. You will find that the mango is more attractive in form than the avocado, and the leaves do not brown as easily.

The Monstera or Swiss-Cheese Plant

Every year the decorating magazines tell us to throw out the old and bring in the new, and it's the same in the world of plants. According to *W* and *HG*—so far *GQ* and *M* have neglected to pass judgment—many once popular horticultural trends are now just as passé as snoods for women, swimtops for men, and iceberg lettuce in a salad. Remember when everyone had an air plant pinned to the living room curtains, and gardeners were happy to have plain white petunias?

If you don't remember those days of yore, you certainly won't recall the popularity that once surrounded the Swiss-cheese plant or *Monstera deliciosa*. During the fifties, every home with any pretense to style had an orange fiberglass tub with a rounded bottom, held aloft in a polished brass ring set with polished brass legs and containing one of these plants, trained to climb up a cedar slab or a piece of fence

post. Other common names include: ceriman, breadfruit vine, hurricane plant, Mexican breadfruit, and the fruit-salad plant.

George and Virginie Elbert, in their book *Foliage Plants for Decorating Indoors*, write, "out-of-doors in the tropics they climb to the very tops of trees, creating a giant tapestry of overlapping leaves. Indoors they are being used to some extent in high-ceilinged, sunny and warm, principally southern-oriented displays. Whether they will continue to be is the question, for they are all rampant vines."

The generic name of *Monstera* is Latin for strange or monstrous and points to some of the oddities associated with this plant, including long and twisting aerial roots that usually never touch ground, large glossy leaves full of holes and deeply lobed cutouts (hence the common name), and edible fruits that look like white pine cones and taste like pineapples. No one has ever proved why the leaves are full of holes, but it has been suggested that heavy tropical rains could drain without causing undue damage, or hurricane winds would whistle right through.

And rampant vines they are, too. That's the reason that I always keep one such plant around. The three-foot glossy green leaves are very attractive, especially against a white wall or twining around a window with partial shade or diffused sunlight.

This plant has a juvenile form whose leaves are split but have not yet developed the holes. This form is known incorrectly as *Philodendron pertusum*.

There is a cultivar available called 'Variegata' that bears irregular light yellow or off-white patches on the leaf, as if a house painter had flung paint dregs at the plant. Eschew it. It is a true horror.

Temperatures should never fall below 55°F, and during the summer months, the

Swiss-Cheese Plant
Monstera deliciosa ▶

soil should be kept evenly moist and the leaves spritzed as often as you can. An excellent soil mix is one-third each good potting soil, peat moss, and sand.

Propagation is by stem cuttings, which include two or more segments or buds, taken any time of the year. They should be set in a warm, sandy compost of at least 70°F. Seed, when available, will also germinate with ease if started in a warm place.

Ever so often a happy plant will flower and fruit. The flowers are very small and crisscross a greenish yellow spadix that is enclosed in a white, waxy spathe, resembling a calla lily or a white jack-in-the-pulpit—not surprising since they all belong to the Araceae family. Over a period of a year or more, the spadix begins to resemble a large ear of corn, turns yellow, and the covering scales fall away. The fruit is eaten fresh in the tropics.

The Ever-Popular Avocado

Amazingly enough, I've never seen an avocado plant offered by any nursery that sells houseplants. The only source is to buy an alligator pear at the local supermarket, use the fruit for lunch, and keep the pit for germination and eventually a tree. The botanical name is *Persea americana*, named after a tree of ancient Egypt and Persia. The avocado originally came from Central America. The fruit has high nutritional value.

After lunch, wash a pit in warm water to remove as much of the surrounding skin as possible. You will often find the pit has already split in preparation for producing a root and soon a stem.

Fill a juice glass with tepid water. Dry the pit, and about a third of the way up from the base—the larger, flat end—force in the first of four toothpicks, half its length into the pit. Space the toothpicks equally around the circumference. Now put the toothpicked pit on the rim of the glass, letting about a half-inch of water cover the pit's base.

Put the glass in a warm place, away from direct sunlight, and keep the water level up at all times. Usually within a week or so, a root tip will begin to emerge from the bottom of the pit. If the water becomes cloudy and the pit begins to decay, throw it out and begin again.

Soon the pit splits entirely, and a green shoot arises with tiny leaves at the tip. Now comes the hard part. To check the soon-to-be-rapid growth of the plant, and to ensure plentiful branching, cut off the growing tip when the stem reaches a height of six inches, leaving about three inches of stem when you are finished. Don't worry. Within a week or so, a new shoot will appear.

Pot the pit when the glass is full of roots and about two weeks after you have cut back the main stem. The pot should be clay and eight inches across at the top. Crock the hole with a pot shard or stone, and use a soil mix of good potting soil, composted manure, peat moss, and sand, one-quarter each. Position the pit so its tip is even with the top of the pot, and add soil until only the pit's top half is exposed.

When the stem reaches a height of sixteen inches, add a ⅝-inch wooden dowel to the pot for future support for the developing trunk.

Give your tree as much sun as you can, and water well as soon as the soil begins to dry. Keep temperatures above 50°F. Fertilize every three months whenever the tree is in active growth.

When the tree reaches a height of six feet, move it into a bigger pot. The next best home is a wooden redwood tub, the kind with brass stays.

If the humidity is low in your home, spritz the leaves with a mister, preferably every day during the summer. Leaves often brown around the edge because of a lack of moisture in the air.

Watch out for spider mites. They are partial to avocado leaves.

Avocados that are grown for produce come from specific varieties that are developed for improved fruit and usually are reproduced by grafting. If your tree is grown from a pit, there is no guarantee that it will bear decent fruit or, for that matter, any fruit at all. It takes about seven years for a tree to flower.

The Flax Lilies

There are only two species of the flax lilies, and both come from New Zealand. The genus is *Phormium* and means basket or wickerwork because baskets, floor mats, sunshades, and rope are woven from the fibers of one species. In their native country, they are often found on poorly drained and peaty areas of mixed tussock grassland, 4,500 feet up in the mountains, not far above the tree line. It is said that the plants reshoot quickly after burning and, like many pines and grasses in the United States, may increase after a forest fire.

The mountain flax bears fairly stiff leaves up to seven feet high of either a deep maroon or deep green, sometimes fading to red with age. Originally called *Phormium Cookianum* after the famous Captain Cook, today the plants are known as *P. Colensoi* after William Colenso (1811–1899), New Zealand's most famous botanist. Colenso was originally a printer from Cornwall who went to the island, translated the New

Testament into the Maori language, and then, with a portable printing press, distributed copies to the local inhabitants. He became a deacon, but after losing his office in 1852 for fathering an illegitimate child, he retired to a farm but never ceased to botanize.

The second species is New Zealand hemp or *Phormium tenax* (*tenax* is Latin for tough and tenacious), the plant used for weaving. Because seedling plants vary a great deal in habit, this species is responsible for a number of colorful and unique cultivars. The leaves are much stiffer than on the mountain flax and can reach nine feet, growing in fans that sit on top of heavy stems, eventually attaining a height of fifteen feet.

The flowers of both species are dull red or yellow and stand in erect panicles. They are more interesting than beautiful to look at. Plants rarely flower in pots.

Phormiums are only hardy to 20°F and must be moved inside every fall in much of the United States. Rather than dig the plants up every fall for the move indoors, I grow them in self-watering pots and dot them around the perennial border for marvelous color accents. At one time in England, these plants were frequently set out in large tubs for garden and conservatory decoration, but they fell out of fashion.

A good soil mix consists of one-quarter each potting soil, peat moss, composted manure, and sand. Temperatures should be cool, usually 50°–65°F with maximum sun. Alfred Byrd Graf, in his valuable *Exotic Plant Manual*, writes of seeing these plants growing right in the cold waters of the southern lakes, and because of this hint, I planted mine in the self-watering pots. Fertilize once in the spring and once in late summer.

The cultivars of *Phormium tenax* are legion, but look for 'Variegatum', with

leaves striped with white and creamy yellow; 'Dazzler', bearing two-inch-wide magenta- and chocolate-striped leaves; 'Apricot Queen', with a leaf combination of yellow and cream with green stripes and red edges; and 'Surfrider', with narrow, twisted leaves of orange and green. 'Bronze Baby' or the dwarf flax has leaves of bronze-purple with coppery edges.

Propagation of the species is by seed, but it loses its viability inside of a year. Vegetative propagation—with these plants the only way to keep a cultivar pure—is by division of the plant into single fans or groups of two or three, discarding any with flower spikes and making sure that each fan has at least four leaves. The old roots die, but new roots quickly form. Vegetative propagation is best accomplished in early spring before new growth begins.

The Mother-of-Thousands

Remember the song "Give me some men who are stout-hearted men, and I'll soon give you ten thousand more"? The mother-of-thousands answers that call, only instead of men, you will get an endless supply of tiny plants. Other common names of this plant are strawberry geranium, beefsteak geranium, strawberry begonia, and creeping-sailor.

The botanical name is *Saxifraga stolonifera*, with the genus coming from the Latin *saxum*, or stone, and *frangere*, meaning to break or fragment. This is a fairly truthful name, since many members of the genus literally live on the surface of rocks—although the weather is responsible for the initial breaks in the rock—taking advantage of every tiny nook and cranny, into which they send their roots in a search

for food, water, and a secure foothold. The species name refers to the many red threads or stolons that come from the mother plant and eventually give rise to the plantlets. Older books call this plant *S. sarmentosa*, and here the species name means "with long, slender runners."

It is interesting to note that this particular plant originally came from China in the collections of one Benjamin Torin. He is seldom remembered today, but back in 1770 one of his consignments that went to London's Kew Gardens contained the strawberry geranium. Some books claim that Robert Fortune brought the plant back from Japan in 1863, but he was almost one hundred years too late.

The leaves are oval, between two and three inches wide, and resemble those of a geranium. The veins are edged with silver and covered with a sparse network of silvery hairs; hence the reference to a begonia. Underneath, the surface is dotted with tiny ovals of dark pink.

My plant began this spring as a plantlet about two inches across and by August was happily growing in a four-inch pot, with twenty-one runners in lengths from nine inches to almost two feet. Most of the runners boast tiny clones to the mother plant above. The white flowers appear in spring on six-inch stalks. They are charming, about one inch across, with two petals much longer than the others.

Soil should be one-quarter each of potting soil, composted manure, peat moss, and sand. Since this plant is hardy outdoors to USDA Zone 6 and yet will live comfortably in a pot in the window, it prefers to be kept cool, with temperatures below 80° in the summer and usually 50°–65°F the rest of the year. Give as much sunlight as possible, and let the soil dry between waterings—but don't forget to water at that point, or some of the stolons will shrivel and dry. Propagation is by

◀ New Zealand Hemp
Phormium tenax

placing a new plantlet in a tiny pot and, when established, cutting the stolon.

Saxifraga stolonifera 'Tricolor', or the variegated strawberry geranium, has striking green-and-white foliage with pink edges. *S. cuscutiformis* is a closely allied species that has smaller leaves veined with white.

The Indoor Linden

According to *Hortus Third*, there are three species of the genus *Sparmannia*. All are shrubs in their native South Africa, and one makes an excellent plant for the home. The genus is named in honor of a Swedish traveler, Dr. Anders Sparrman (1748–1820), who accompanied Captain Cook on his second voyage.

The plant usually grown in containers is *Sparmannia africana*, called the African hemp because it is a source of fibers used in making cloth and the indoor linden because the leaves resemble those of the linden tree (*Tilia spp.*). They are very popular plants in Europe and found in many sunny window gardens.

The large, soft leaves are angled and lobed, up to eight inches long, and covered with a silky down. Even the stems still retain a few silky hairs long after their surface has turned to bark.

These are fast-growing plants, usually flowering when only two feet high but continuing to grow up to eight feet in the home and fifteen to twenty feet outside in a USDA Zone 9 climate. Temperatures in the winter should never fall below 50°F, with 60°F an ideal temperature. If they grow too quickly, they can be cut back, and new shoots will appear. Many gardeners take three- to four-inch cuttings in early spring and begin with new plants every two years. Sometimes seed is offered from the nurseries that deal in rarer plants. If you want a large plant, repot one each spring.

Soil should be one-third each of potting soil, peat moss, and composted manure. Provide full sun for most of the year, but during July and August, partial shade is best. Keep the soil evenly moist from April until October, cutting back on water during the winter months. Feed plants every month during periods of active growth.

The white flowers appear in many-flowered umbels in midspring. Each blossom is about one inch wide, with four petals and four smaller sepals surrounding a large collection of purple-tipped stamens at the center. The sensitive stamens are interesting, moving outward when brushed by a finger or touched by a gentle breeze.

Sparmannia africana 'Flore Pleno' bears double flowers. *S. africana* 'Variegata' has white areas on the leaves.

The Inch Plants

Up until a few years ago, many of the inch plants were generally given the name of wandering Jew. This common name came from a literary and popular legend that began some five hundred years ago and referred to the plant's habit of trailing along or cascading down from a pot, growing older with a longer and longer stem, never rooting along the way, but eventually being rejuvenated by cuttings and beginning to wander again.

According to the *Columbia Encyclopedia*, this myth, which saw its beginnings in the prejudice of the sixteenth century, concerned "a Jew who mocked or mistreated Jesus while He was on His way to the cross and who was condemned therefore to a life of wandering on earth until Judgment Day. The story is common in Western Europe, but it presents marked

Mother-of-Thousands
Saxifraga stolonifera

national variations; e.g., in Spanish and Portuguese the Wandering Jew . . . goes about doing good for expiation."

Benét's Reader's Encyclopedia adds that the "Jew is periodically rejuvenated to the age of thirty [but] his character changes, however; he is now extremely wise, and, in his repentance, he uses the time of his wandering to exhort other men to be mindful of their sins and avoid the wrath of God."

These various plant members of the Commelinaceae or spiderwort family could well have been called the Cain plant, since he was the first human being to suffer such a curse, or perhaps the Flying Dutchman plant, but literary references to the character ranged from Goethe, Eugène Sue (who wrote sensational romances in early-eighteenth-century France), and Shelley in *Queen Mab*, so until today the literary appellation was used. Today there is a move to change the common name from wandering Jew to inch plant, which would apply to all the plants with this growth habit.

The five plants described in this chapter are all excellent for the hanging basket or pot. Even though they flower with charming three-petaled blossoms, their beauty is in the leaves. The one fault is that, as they age, they lose their older leaves, eventually becoming all stems with just a knot of leaves at the tip. So to have the most attractive plants, frequently start them anew from cuttings, as they root easily at the nodes on the stem. Most will root in a glass of plain water.

Soil should be one-quarter each of potting soil, composted manure, peat moss, and sand. Water well, then let the soil dry before watering again. Temperatures are best held above 50°F, but individual requirements are given in the discussion of each plant.

The plant that has always been called

the inch plant bears the botanical name of *Callisia congesta variegata*, with the genus from the Greek *kallos*, for beauty. The leaves arise from a sheath around the stem, with the space between each sheath lengthening with age, and at the tip of the stem they grow in a tight whorl. The leaves have wavy edges, are beautifully striped with bands of white, and are suffused with a purple glow both fore and aft. This is an exceptionally fine plant for a hanging basket. Provide partial shade, and keep the soil evenly moist, fertilizing every two months. Temperatures should stay above 60°F.

The bamboo spiderwort bears the botanical name of *Murdannia acutifolia variegata*, *acutifolia* meaning leaves sharpened to a point. This is a new plant on the horticultural scene, and I've been unable to find a reference to the derivation of the genus, but nevertheless, for the indoor garden, this plant is a must. Glossy leaves up to twelve inches long are lined with stripes of white, varying from the width of a penline to a quarter-inch or more. Since the stems have nodes and grow upright, they resemble bamboos. As with most plants in this family, the nodes are flushed with a purple stain. When the stems become too long and bend over, it's time to start new plants from cuttings. Keep temperatures above 55°F.

The giant white inch plant or *Tradescantia albiflora* 'Albovittata' bears three-inch lance-shaped leaves of light green vigorously striped with longitudinal bands of white. Like many of the inch plants, the leaves have a crystalline quality when viewed close up in sunlight. Most of the Commelinaceae bear purple or violet flowers; hence the species name for this plant—its flowers are white, and *albi* is Latin for white. The genus name is in honor of the intrepid English plant explorer John Tradescant.

◀ African Hemp
Sparmannia africana

The white velvet or gossamer plant, *Tradescantia sillamontana*, comes from Mexico and gets its common name from the weblike hairs that cover the surfaces of the leaves and stems. The species name refers to mountains. This plant grows erect and then with time begins to hang. The two-inch leaves are almost olive drab on top and pale purple below, with the usual sparkle of the leaf cut by the cobwebs that surround everything. The three-petaled flowers are orchid purple. Because of the protection from the hairy coat, the gossamer plant revels in full sun. Let the soil dry completely before watering.

Finally there are the inch plants from the genus *Zebrina*, latinized from the Portuguese *zebra*, here referring to the stripes on the leaves. The species is *pendula*. All are effective in hanging baskets. The two-inch-long leaves are fleshy, and the veins of the leaves will sparkle in the light. They all want temperatures above 50°F.

Zebrina pendula is the most common. The purple leaves are striped with silver, and stems bear rosy purple flowers. The plant is very tolerant and will grow in bright sun to filtered shade. *Zebrina pendula* 'Daniel's Hybrid' has all-purple leaves.

The Mallet Flower

A number of the plants in my collection are from the tropics, mainly because these particular specimens are happy with warm temperatures all year long and rarely drop leaves. In fact, the only sign they give to a year's passing is to go into a dormant phase—usually in the winter if they are from the Northern Hemisphere and in the summer if their home is below the Equator.

A plant from the latter group is the mallet flower or *Tupidanthus calyptratus*. The genus reflects the common name, because *tupis* is Latin for mallet, and *anthos* is flower. The species name means having a calyptra or cap, referring again to the flower structure. There is only one species in the genus, and it hails from India and Cambodia and was introduced into England in 1856.

The compound leaves consist of seven to nine leaflets, each up to one foot in length, and hang from the end of a fourteen-inch stalk. The flowers are described as greenish and occurring in umbels.

My wife has worked for a number of years in our local library. Last April the volunteers became particularly involved with cleaning things up, and she brought home a dusty and forlorn-looking plant literally hanging over the edge of a ten-inch fiberglass bucket that itself perched on three brass-plated legs. The leaves were dusty and bespotted with flyspecks. All in all, it was a plant that had seen better days.

"I thought you could fix it up," she said, expressing her faith in my horticultural ministrations and forcing me to take the challenge.

Because the plant was so bent over, it gave no hint that it might be a tree, so my first searches for nomenclature were incorrect. But finally I learned it was a *Tupidanthus* and immediately propped up the stem and replanted it in an eight-inch self-watering pot. So many of the roots had perished that here was a case of potting down, not up. It now stood three feet high.

I used a mix of potting soil, peat moss, composted manure, and sand, one-quarter each. Then I washed all the leaves with soap and water, rinsing carefully, and by so doing removed a year or more of grime. I set it in a south window with an outside screen for its first associations with sunlight.

By June new growth had appeared at the top, and by the end of August the tree

Inch Plant ►
Callisia congesta variegata

stood at five feet, with a new leaf appearing every three weeks or so.

I've been informed that a mallet flower can reach a height of twelve feet indoors and is a stunning decorator plant. It also can take a great deal of punishment and recover with a grand showing.

PART THREE

ORNAMENTAL GRASSES

Ornamental grasses have long been popular with many gardeners. but in the past few years they have suddenly hit the big time. There is good reason, for the plants are attractive in growth, produce interesting and often beautiful plumes of flowers, and require little upkeep. But few gardeners realize that a number of the grasses make marvelous houseplants.

The following plants include bamboos, grasses—both members of the same family—and a number of grasslike plants, including sedges and the prehistoric horsetail.

The Bamboos

When thinking of bamboos, I usually envision steamy jungles with orange orangutans crawling beneath masses of pendulous foliage that hide Chinese robber barons who are at war with Malayan rubber pirates, or cute pandas with their paws full of bamboo salad—but never gardens in suburban New Jersey or clay pots in Manhattan. However, many of the ornamental bamboos are hardy in USDA Zone 4. Of these, at least a dozen species make excellent container plants for indoor gardening.

In the Orient, bamboo has centuries of tradition behind it and has literally served in everything from banquets to buildings. The young sprouts of several species are considered a delicacy, and construction projects, especially in Japan, rely on bamboo scaffolding in lieu of metal. The Chinese, not to be outdone, have used pulped bamboo as a major source of paper for centuries.

All the continents except Europe have native bamboos. In America we have the giant southern cane (*Arundinaria gigantea*), which grows from southern Ohio to Oklahoma and then south to the Gulf of Mexico, and a subspecies, switch cane (*A. gigantea* subsp. *tecta*), which grows along the Atlantic coast south to Maryland.

Bamboos and grasses are both members of the Gramineae, and the difference between the plants is one of quality, not quantity. Both share the same structural elements—although bamboos are a bit more primitive in the evolutionary sense.

The culms, or stems, are very woody and are extensions of a complex and well-developed system of rhizomes, which wander about underground for many feet and give bamboos the reputation for being aggressive in the garden. There is also a pronounced culm node that corresponds to the knot on a grass stem.

Some bamboos are monocarpic: they live only a short time after flowering. Other species seem to be in continual flowering, but the majority fall between these two extremes. The tropical varieties tend to be more monocarpic than those of the north, and a most interesting fact is that all clones of a particular species of bamboo will flower at the same time regardless of where they are in the world—this last habit causing grief to the Chinese panda.

All bamboos when brought indoors will need a spot with plenty of bright light and yet shaded from the hot suns of summer. Temperatures must not be too high; in fact, most prefer temperatures of 50°–65°F, better than average humidity, and a good, evenly moist soil. Fluctuations in these last two requirements plus cold drafts in winter will cause many plants to drop their leaves. The best all-around soil mix is potting soil, peat moss, and sand, one-third each. Fertilize only in early spring, midsummer, and early fall as a partial check on overactive growth. Propagation is by division.

Warning: If you are planting bamboos outdoors in the landscape south of USDA Zone 5, make sure you install a barrier below ground level to keep the rhizomes from spreading throughout your garden. Bamboos are extremely invasive.

THE PYGMY BAMBOO

The smallest of the cultivated bamboos is the pygmy bamboo. Its botanical name is *Arundinaria pygmaea*—*arundo* is Latin for a reed or cane—but many books persist in calling it *Sasa pygmaea*, with *sasa* being a Japanese name for dwarf bamboos. This plant is an attractive addition to a dish garden and looks especially good in a clay pot or one decorated with an oriental motif. It also makes an excellent ground cover

Bamboos ▶
Arundinaria viridistriata and *A. pygmaea*

outdoors and, unlike many bamboos, can be kept in check with a lawn mower.

Interestingly, pygmy bamboo leaves do not fold up when cut for a flower arrangement, while the leaves of other bamboos will. Stems stay between ten and fourteen inches high.

THE DWARF WHITE-STRIPE BAMBOO

The dwarf white-stripe bamboo or *Arundinaria variegata* bears small leaves striped with creamy white and is also an excellent candidate for a dish garden. This plant was brought back from Japan by Robert Fortune in 1862, and older books still list it as *A. Fortunei*. Outside the stems can reach a height of three feet, but indoors they stay about one foot high.

THE KAMURO-ZASA BAMBOO

The bamboo that has the most beautiful leaf color is the kamuro-zasa bamboo. Its botanical name is *Arundinaria viridistriata*; the species is Latin for striped with green. The Japanese name is Kamuro-zasa, and older books still call it *Pleioblastus viridistriatus*, with the genus being Greek for many shoots. The leaves are difficult to describe: they have a velvety look when new, and the golden and green tones meld together from a distance. Stems are between two and three feet high.

THE BLACK BAMBOO

Although it sounds like a cliché, the black bamboo is deservedly called the "jewel of the bamboos" with its bright green leaves and jet black culms. Originally from southern China, the black bamboo is known as the Whangee or Wangee cane and was brought to England in 1823.

Culms will reach a height of twenty-five feet when outside but usually stop at about ten feet when grown in containers. Black bamboo needs good light but prefers some shade from very hot afternoon sun. When new, the culms are green and speckled with black, but they become solid black with age. Many older references list this bamboo as *Phyllostachys bambusa*, with the genus meaning spiked leaf but the correct name is *P. nigra*.

True Ornamental Grasses

The following three plants are all true members of the grass family. They originate in the tropics and so are very happy in warm rooms and sunny windows.

THE BASKET GRASS

Basket grass is one of the few grasses that is suited to be both a potted plant and an excellent choice for a hanging basket. The genus is *Oplismenus*, from *oplismenos*, meaning armored, referring to the sparse but spikelike blooming panicle. The species name is *hirtellus*, meaning somewhat hairy, an unfair designation, since the hairiness is so slight as to be nonexistent and only visible in the bloom. According to the *Royal Horticultural Society Dictionary of Gardening* basket grass arrived in England from New Caledonia in 1867, but *Hortus Third* claims it to be native from Texas, through Mexico and the West Indies, and down to Argentina.

The cultivar usually found in cultivation is 'Variegatus', and this variety bears white and pinkish purple striped leaves that almost sparkle as long as the plant gets plenty of sun and water. During active growth, it should be fed only every few months.

Soil should be one-third each of

Basket Grass
Oplismenus hirtellus

potting soil, peat moss, and sand. The temperature should always be above 55°F, and basket grass needs high humidity, so remember to spritz the leaves every day. The stems root at the nodes—obvious knots or swellings on the stems—so to propagate, simply push a node into the dirt, and hold it down with a small stone or a bobby pin.

Basket grass is used as a ground cover in tropical countries, and it's very effective in an outdoor planter when twined around a central display of a more upright plant, like a canna or a cabbage palm seedling.

Many grasses can fall prey to spider mites, especially in low humidity. If you have trouble with this pest, try washing the leaves with soap and water every few days for a week or two.

Keep the soil evenly moist, but if you forget to water and the plant dries, or if the mites are too much, shear the stems back to the surface. The grass will sprout anew.

THE BEAUTIFUL PALM GRASS

About six years ago, I received seed of palm grass, *Setaria palmifolia*, from a correspondent in the Canary Islands. I had been looking for this particular grass for many years before that unexpected gift, because written descriptions in a number of old books dealing with greenhouse plants called it a magnificent and beautiful addition to the conservatory.

A number of the species in this genus are used for food, and foxtail millet, *Setaria italica*, has been cultivated since prehistoric times. The genus is from the Latin *seta*, a bristle, and refers to the numerous bristles on the flowerheads.

Originally found growing in rocky woods and banks in southeastern Asia and India, foxtail millet was introduced into Jamaica and the southern United States as an ornamental. Called a robust perennial, in its original Southeast Asian home it usually

grows in damp, shady situations in altitudes from sea level up to six thousand feet. A few references cite the grain as being eaten as a substitute for rice and the tender shoots as a vegetable, but usually it is written as being entirely an ornamental. The emerald green blades are plaited, about 20 inches long and 2⅜ inches wide on stems up to 6 feet tall.

There is a variegated form called *niveo-vittatum* and introduced by Messrs. Veitch and Son of England in 1868. Its long, deep green leaves are striped with white with a touch of pink along the edges. But in all my searches, I've never found this particular plant.

Soil should be kept evenly moist, and I keep my plant in an eight-inch self-watering pot. The soil mix is one-third each of potting soil, composted manure, and sand. Temperatures should not fall below 55°F (although occasional lapses to 50°F seem to do no harm). Fertilize every few months while the plants are in active growth.

Graceful panicles of seeds appear in early summer and stay on the plant throughout the year.

Propagation is by division in early spring or by seed.

FRESH-SMELLING LEMONGRASS

Southern Florida, parts of California, and Hawaii are the only states where it is warm enough to grow lemongrass out-of-doors. But it does very well as a houseplant in the rest of the country and becomes a faithful specimen plant if you leave it outside for the summer, always giving it as much sun as possible.

The botanical name is *Cymbopogon citratus*, and the genus is derived from the Greek *kumbe*, or boat, and *pogon*, or beard, alluding to the boat-shaped spathes. The

Palm Grass
Setaria palmifolia ▶

plant usually grown in commerce is a cultigen that seldom flowers.

The grass rarely tops four feet in a pot but can go well over six feet in the tropics. The leaves are one of the commercial sources of lemon oil, and it's always a great conversation piece when you ask visitors to crush a bit of leaf between their fingers and inhale the bright, fresh smell of lemons. Hence the species name of *citratus*.

Other members of the *Cymbopogons* are used in commerce. *Cymbopogon flexuosus* produces Malabar grass oil, another lemon flavor; *C. martinii* is the source of ginger-grass oil; while *C. Nardus* and *C. winterianus* yield citronella oil. A number of species are said to have medicinal value, and *C. Nardus* is used in the manufacture of paper pulp.

But there is another use for this grass: it's one of the main food flavorings in most cooking from Thailand, where the plant is called *takrai*. It's either grown in the Thai home or purchased both fresh and dried from neighborhood markets. Occasionally the dried form is found in the spice section at larger supermarkets in America.

The following recipe, while somewhat hot to American taste, is absolutely delicious. In addition to the lemongrass, you will need fish sauce or *nam pla*, available in most of the larger gourmet shops.

SHRIMP SOUP WITH LEMONGRASS
(4 to 6 servings)

1½ quarts chicken broth
1 tablespoon dried lemongrass, torn into small
    pieces
⅛ teaspoon hot-pepper seeds (or to taste)
Juice of one large lemon
Dash *nam pla* (fish sauce)
½ pound raw, small, shelled shrimps, deveined
3–4 green onions, chopped
5–6 sprigs fresh or dried coriander

Bring the broth to a boil in a saucepan, and drop in the lemongrass. Continue to boil for five minutes, then add pepper seeds, lemon juice, and fish sauce. Lower heat, and add the shrimps. Cook three or four minutes until the shrimps are opaque and pink. Add green onions and coriander. Serve at once.

The leaves grow from a swollen node that almost resembles a bulb, and this node can be sliced in very thin sections and floated in almost any clear soup or broth.

To grow lemongrass, use a soil mix of potting soil, composted manure, and sand, one-third each. A self-watering pot is a good idea, since lemongrass wants an evenly moist soil at all times. Fertilize every month during the summer.

The Grasslike Sedges

Sedges are grasslike herbs that belong to the family Cyperaceae. The true sedges belong to the genus *Carex*, of which there are well over five hundred species. The genus is from the Greek *keiro*, or cut, and refers to the many species whose leaves have very sharp edges. Sedges are easily identified from grasses by their three-ranked leaves, often rolled and threadlike, and their triangular stems that are solid rather than hollow and all having a pithy center. While the sedges lack brightly colored flowers, they still possess stamens and pistils, and they produce tiny, leathery nuts as seeds.

While a few sedges grow on dry ground, most are plants of cool and temperate regions that revel in swamps, pool borders, ditches, riverbanks, and marshes. Here they form an intermediate step between useless (to humans) mud and valuable dry land by spreading their rhizomes and acting as a landfill that eventually allows other vegetation to grow.

A good soil mix is one-third each of potting soil, peat moss, and sand. Sedges are all good candidates for self-watering pots,

Carex Morrowii and
C. phyllocephala 'Sparkler' ▶

as the soil should be kept evenly moist at all times. Temperatures should be cool, usually 50°–65°F. Fertilize only a few times a year and then only when plants are in active growth. Full sun is good except in the hot months of summer, when partial shade is best.

A SEDGE SELECTION

The leatherleaf or Buchanan's sedge, *Carex buchanani*, bears leaves that are round in cross section and taper to a curled point, with this delicate form matched to an attractive red-brown color. Leaves are about one foot long. Although originally from New Zealand, this sedge has an oriental look to it and is especially effective as a decorator plant. Outdoors it is hardy to about 10°F and needs a winter mulch for protection.

The miniature variegated sedge, *Carex foliosissima* 'Albomediana', is a tufted plant with narrow six-inch flat leaves about a quarter-inch wide. The leaves are bright green with a white stripe near each margin, growing stiffly erect.

Japanese sedge grass, *Carex Morrowii* var. *expallida*, is one of the most popular ornamental grasses and is found in almost every major nursery catalog of the last decade. The gracefully arched leaves are a shiny green striped with creamy white. In climates south of Philadelphia, the leaves are green all winter.

This is also an excellent pot plant. If given adequate light and cool winters, it will bloom in early spring, producing flowers that resemble crushed camel-hair brushes that have been dipped in bright yellow powder.

Another sedge originally from China and now cultivated in Japan is *Tenjiku-suge* or *Carex phyllocephala*—the species title refers to the way the leaves grow from a central point, with *phyllo* meaning leaf and *cephala* meaning head. I first saw the plant growing in the Temperate House of the Brooklyn Botanic Garden. This was a variegated form with the cultivar name of 'Sparkler'. About one foot tall, it has purplish sheaths at the base of each tufted head of the leaf blades, with each leaf margined and striped with ivory white. All in all, it's a most attractive plant. Word has it that this plant is hardy in USDA Zone 6.

The Egyptian Papyrus

The Egyptian papyrus is the same plant that surrounded the baby Moses when he was discovered by Pharaoh's daughter. *Cyperus Papyrus* is a tender perennial that can reach a height of fifteen feet in its native Egypt but usually stays around five feet in a pot and eight feet in a pool setting. *Cyperus* is the ancient Greek name for this important member of the Cyperaceae family.

Also known as the Egyptian paper plant, it's been used in the manufacture of paper since 2700 B.C. The process involves taking thin and wet strips of the pith from flowering stems, laying them so the edges slightly overlap, crossing them by strips similarly arranged, then drying the sheets under weights to make papyrus. *Cyperus* has also seen service as a roof thatching, been distilled for alcohol, and, when tied together in bundles, served as "logs" for a raft. Plants were brought to England from Egypt in 1803.

The basal leaves in this plant have been reduced to small brown sheaths on the triangular stems. What we take to be leaves are really bracts that cluster at the top of the stem and surround spikes that end in the scalelike flowers.

Cyperus can be grown in an indoor or outdoor pool, or in a pot set in a larger container so the rhizomes are always under water.

Papyrus ▶
Cyperus Papyrus

Temperatures should be kept above 60°F, but I have grown this plant in a cool greenhouse where water temperatures were usually around 50°F.

Start plants in clay pots, and use a soil mix of two parts potting soil, two parts composted manure, and one part sand. If the plant is being set in a pool, stop the soil about one inch from the pot top, and fill the rest with small crushed stone or gravel to keep the dirt from muddying up the water. Either indoors or out, give these plants plenty of sun. Fertilize once in early spring and once in midsummer. Propagation is by seed or division.

The Fiberoptic Plant

Another member of the Cyperaceae that has had great success as a houseplant, especially popular in Europe, is the fiberoptic plant or *Scirpus cernuus*, long known in horticultural circles as *Isolepis gracilis*. The genus is from an old Greek name for a rush first used by Pliny.

The common name is more than apt. The little white flower heads, which resemble white puffs, are found at the tip of each curving stem—the stems look like six-inch green threads—and the plant looks for all the world like one of those novelty lamps advertised in the *National Enquirer*. Other common names are electric grass and fountain bullrush. Grow as papyrus, making sure that the pot is always in a saucer of water.

The Horsetails

Millions of years ago and throughout the Carboniferous Period of geologic time, vast American coalfields were formed as mounds of vegetation sank ever deeper into the mire and through chemical action eventually became deep veins of coal. During this time, dragonflies with fourteen-inch wingspreads flitted about misty swamps among ferns that rose thirty feet into a sky that held scuttling clouds, smoke from volcanoes, and, toward the end, swooping pterodactyls. Spiders, land snails, and scorpions crawled over giant club mosses called calamites, and over eight hundred kinds of cockroaches roamed the earth. And there among the ferns and primitive conifers were the giant horsetails, members of the *Equisetum* genus and even at that time among the oldest plants upon the Earth.

Today the horsetails have diminished in size, the largest rarely topping four feet. The botanical name *Equisetum* is from the Latin, *equus*, a horse, and *seta*, a bristle, and refers to the plant's resemblance to a horse's tail when many of the species produce stems covered with whorled branches.

Equisetum hyemale grows along streams, lakes, ditches, and the edges of old railroad beds. The plant has a stark, architectural beauty all its own and looks especially good in combination with ferns or alone at the water's edge.

The evergreen shoots grow from a perennial rhizome and have such a high silica content that in pioneer days they were used to clean and polish pots and pans. The conelike caps that top the ringed stems produce spores, not seeds, that follow a complicated reproductive cycle like the ferns'. Spores produce small, green, lobed prothalli that manufacture both male and female cells, which eventually meet to form a new plant.

The tiny pennants that circle the rings, which in turn section off the stems, are primitive, scalelike leaves, so the major part of photosynthesis occurs in the stem. Individual stem sections can be pulled apart like poppit beads and put back together again.

Fiberoptic Plant ▶
Scirpus cernuus

Equisetum hyemale does quite well for me in a self-watering pot, where it spends the winter in a sunny but cool place in the window and summers outside at the edge of a small pool in the backyard. I use a soil mix of one part potting soil, one part peat moss, and two parts sand. The plants are never fertilized. The clumps are easily divided in spring.

If you plant them directly in the garden, make sure you section off the area, as these ancient rushes are not too old to be very, very invasive. The rhizomes often grow straight down, reaching a length of three feet, and fragment easily; each piece has the potential to start a new plant.

In addition to the larger types, there are some that remain very small. *Equisetum scirpoides*, or the dwarf scouring rush, is found on open banks and at the edges of coniferous woods from Greenland south to a line extending from New York State west to Washington. The threadlike stems reach a height of three inches and are perfect for miniature gardens and bonsai applications. They also are invasive in the garden.

Equisetum variegatum is so-called because the dark green stems have a pronounced black band on the leaves above each section. These plants grow to six inches.

A Special Cordyline

If the number of common names is any key to popularity, *Cordyline* is very popular indeed. Known as the cabbage palm or cabbage tree, giant dracaena, sword grass, fountain dracaena, palm lily, and the grass palm, it belies popularity, since most people never recognize the name and only know the plant after it's pointed out as the central planting in pots set out by nurseries all over the United States early in the season. You've all seen it: the pot of geraniums or lobelia or the variegated *Vinca major* that creep or hang over the edge of a plastic container, and in the center is a fountain of some fifteen or twenty stiff but gracefully bending thin leaves that reach a height of some fourteen inches. The seedlings are usually grown in three-inch pots in a greenhouse during their first year and will be salable by May of the second year.

This central plant is a seedling of *Cordyline australis*. The genus is from the Greek *kordyle*, or club, referring to the stout roots of some of the species. The species does not refer to the island continent but to the Southern Hemisphere in general.

Originally found in New Zealand in 1860, in nature this plant becomes a tree growing to a height of forty feet with a fountain of the leaves atop a single cylindrical stem, often three feet long and 1 to 2½ inches wide.

Sixteen years ago, at a July clearance sale, I paid ninety-eight cents for a pot of an imaginative arrangement that included this "grass." I repotted this grass in a five-inch pot and brought it indoors before frost. Today the trunk is eight feet high, gives rise to some hundreds of leaves on the top, and sits in a fourteen-inch pot. Soon it will be too heavy to move about, and I'll be forced to cut a hole in the ceiling of the greenhouse so it can continue to thrive.

Quite often English garden books have beautiful photographs of sumptuous gardens that feature the cabbage palm, since it is hardy outdoors south of London. I get the same effect by moving my plant to the border for the summer, where it profits from the fresh air and sunshine.

Use a mix of potting soil, peat moss, and composted manure, and repot every two years or so. Cabbage palms respond beautifully to root pruning, so if your plant is potbound, try cutting back the roots in the spring. Give it plenty of water during the summer, and reduce watering only

◀ Horsetails
Equisetum hyemale

when the plant is dormant during the dead of winter.

Cabbage palm is said to flower with creamy white, fragrant flowers and produce a white or bluish berry, but I doubt this happens to a containerized tree.

There are a number of cultivars, including 'Atropurpurea', whose leaves have a purple midrib, and 'Doucetii', which has leaves striped and edged with white.

Watch out for spider mites!

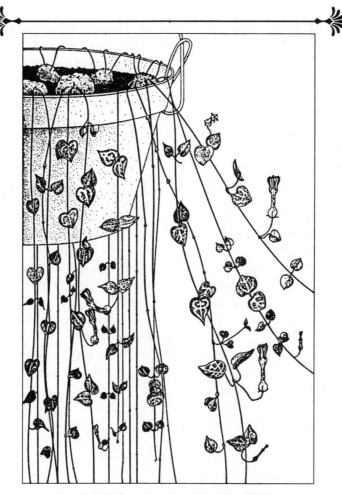

PART FOUR

VINES

Not all plants are content to stay close to the earth and put a large share of their energies into stem growth in order to get their place in the sun. The vines found a different way, using various methods ranging from winding their stems around another plant's trunk or developing curling tendrils like a grape to grasp a support, to actually leaning on neighboring plants. This last group of vines will grow through or over other plants, eventually flopping their way to the sky.

The vines in this book are quite at home in or around a window. Folding trellises are available from suppliers, or you can achieve wonders with fishing line or plastic twine wound around the windowsill, sash, and frame.

The Calico Flowers

The birthworts (*wort* is an Old English word for plant) are members of the *Aristolochia* genus. The name comes from the Greek *aristos*, best, and *lochia*, meaning childbirth, referring to the use of this plant as a medicine and a specific against plague. In his 1597 version of the *Herball*, John Gerard wrote, "Dioscorides writeth that a dram weight of long birthwort drunk with wine and so applied is good against serpents and deadly things." One wonders which ingredient was the most effective.

Most birthworts are greenhouse plants and indoor vines, but one—*A. durior* or Dutchman's-pipe—is hardy in the north and used as a quick-covering vine for screens and porches.

The most bizarre is the pelican flower, *Aristolochia gigantea*, arriving in England from Guatemala in 1841. A high-climbing vine reaching ten feet in length, it bears flat, smooth, heart-shaped leaves that have a rank odor when crushed. The six-inch flowers are off-white, veined with purple, and sit atop a U-shaped, inflated, greenish tube and bear an unattractive odor. But as flowers they are showstoppers.

The vines are best in pots that hang on wires allowing plenty of room for growth. They can also be carefully unwound from one wire and rewound on another, making counterclockwise turns.

The calico flower, *Aristolochia elegans*, is less peculiar and almost cute. It was exported from Brazil in 1883 and is a free-flowering species once it's settled in. Its flowers are 1½ inches long and 3 inches wide, with a yellow tube and purple flaps marked with white. As a vine, it's shorter than the pelican, reaching only eight feet in length.

Both of these plants want warm surroundings with temperatures always above 60°F. A good soil mix is one-quarter each of potting soil, peat moss, composted manure, and sand. Keep the soil evenly moist but never soggy, and give the vine a spot in partial shade, as hot summer sun can burn the leaves.

Propagation is by cuttings or by seed.

The Climbing Onion

An English gardener by the name of E. A. Bowles had an area of his garden that he called the Lunatic Asylum, where he kept plants that had strange growth patterns, weird flowers, or unsettling ways about them. If it were a hardy plant, I'm sure the climbing onion or, as it's often called, the Zulu potato would have been given a front seat in Bowles's collection.

Known botanically as *Bowiea volubilis*, the genus is in honor of J. Bowie (1789–1869), a plant collector who was said to have spent a lot of his time in London bar-parlours telling apocryphal stories of his Brazilian and Cape Town adventures instead of working in the field. But apparently he did bring back this unusual plant from South Africa. *Volubilis* is Latin for twining.

Some years ago, a houseplant aficionado sent me a green ball, four inches in diameter, with a slight depression that marked the top and a few dried rootlets that signified the bottom. The accompanying letter advised me to plant it in a five-inch pot with a soil mix of one-third each potting soil, composted manure, and sand, placing the top half of the bulb above the soil line. "Water it after the growth begins," wrote my correspondent, "and let the soil dry out between waterings. Growth will die back in late spring or fall depending on when you have started the plant. Keep temperatures above 50°F and fertilize once a month while it's growing."

Calico Flower
Aristolochia elegans ▶

I followed the directions and was soon rewarded by twining stems, ⅝-inch-wide starlike green flowers, and minuscule leaves represented by tiny triangular flaps of green where the branchlets grow from the branch.

A spot in partial sun is best, and my bulb sat for years with its clay pot set inside a Japanese basket so the foliage had something to cling to. A healthy bulb will eventually reach a diameter of eight inches with a corresponding increase in stem production.

Propagation is by seed and sometimes by offset bulbs.

The Rosary Vine

A few plants in the window-garden lexicon live up to their reputation for toughness. The aspidistra and the sansevieria come to mind, but in my experience one of the long-distance runners is the rosary vine. My sister-in-law gave me this plant in 1982: it's never been repotted, I continually forget to water it, it's suffered both heat and cold, and it still fights on—and blooms!

The botanical name is *Ceropegia Woodii*, with the genus coming from the Greek *keros*, for wax, and *pege*, a fountain, supposedly referring to the flower's waxy appearance but one of the more farfetched attempts at appellation that I've run across. Although it's not too obvious, these plants belong to the same family as the stapelias (which see). The species is named in honor of John Medley Wood (1827–1915), who retired from the East Indian Merchant Service and began collecting native African plants. He is also the man who introduced sugarcane into Natal.

Originally from Natal and southern Rhodesia, the plant has pairs of succulent heart-shaped leaves, less than one inch wide, that run along thin, threadlike purple stems that arise from little tubers and trail or hang according to their method of planting. Because of these tubers, the plant has the ability to store water over a long period of time. Among the common names are rosary vine, hearts-on-a-string, string-of-hearts, and hearts-entangled, this last because the stems easily become enmeshed and wound up together, taking a great deal of patience to straighten out.

The inch-long flowers have a round base with a tubular projection that is topped with a tiny parachute covered on its interior with a black fringe. They appear at odd times throughout the year. The little tubers that appear at the internodes on the stems are used to start new plants.

Use a soil mix of one-third each potting soil, peat moss, and sand, and plant the tubers with one-half above the soil line. Water only when the soil is dry, and give the plants a spot in partial sun. Fertilize only once or twice a year.

Propagation is by using the stem tubers, cuttings, or sometimes seeds, but the flowers are rarely fertilized when growing indoors. If they are, it's probably a fly that does the job.

The Wax Plant

Remember "Tzena, Tzena, Tzena," Gordon Jenkin's arrangement of a traditional Yiddish folk song that became one of the million bestseller hits of 1950? The tune always comes to my mind when I think of the wax plant, but the title becomes *Hoya, Hoya, Hoya*.

The genus *Hoya* is named in honor of Thomas Hoy, one-time gardener to the Duke of Northumberland at Sion House in England, and represents some two hundred species of root-climbing and twining plants

Climbing Onion
Bowiea volubilis

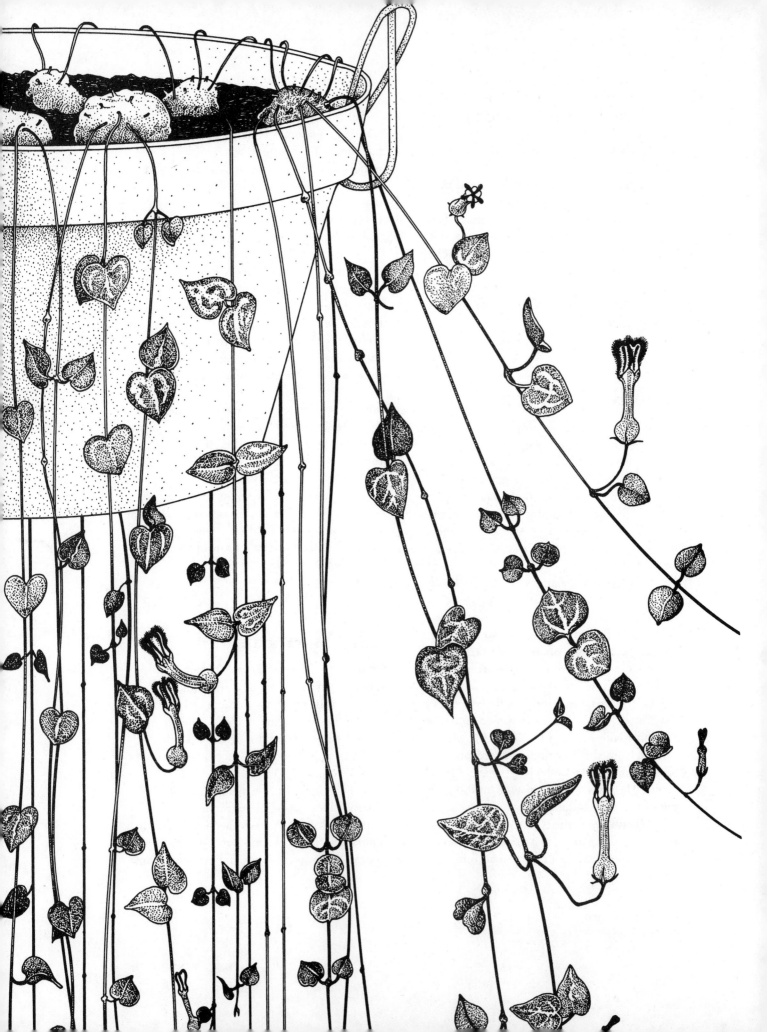

with three-inch fleshy and succulent leaves plus bunches of exotic flowers. They belong to the Asclepiadaceae family along with the rosary vine and the stapelias.

The plants usually found in unsophisticated collections are *Hoya carnosa* and *H. bella*. In the first, the species name means fleshy and refers to the color of the waxy blossoms; in the second, it means beautiful. But many indoor gardeners become so enamored of these plants that they turn to lesser-known species, and there is now a Hoya Society International, Logee's keeps fifteen hoyas in its catalog, and Glasshouse Works lists thirty-three.

For years I kept a *Hoya carnosa* in a large clay pot held to a chain by a wire clip. Even though the silver-speckled, deep green leaves were abundant and healthy, the plant never looked quite right to me. So two years ago I moved it and two more plants to a twelve-inch wire basket lined with a sheet of sphagnum moss.

After a month or so of settling in, they began to grow, sending out many curling and climbing stems that wound about the three chains holding the planter. One of the good things about wax plants is that you can unwind a stem if its direction doesn't please you, and wind it about somewhere else. Just make sure you wind the stems in a counterclockwise direction.

The soil mix I use is one-third each of potting soil, peat moss, and sand, because these plants need perfect drainage. Temperatures should be temperate, but never let them fall below 50°F (although *Hoya carnosa* will tolerate 45° for a short time). Keep the soil on the dry side when plants are in growth, but remember to withhold watering during the winter months, adding water only if the leaves begin to shrink and shrivel. Then make sure the water is tepid. Fertilize them once in the spring and only after the plants have been established for at least a year. These plants do not do well in rich soil.

Another point to remember is never to remove the peduncle, or flower stalk, as new buds will set on the same old spur, and you can count the passing of the years by the length of the stalk. Once the plant is in bud, do not move the container, as the change in light direction can impede the development of the flower.

Each of the star-shaped flowers—appearing anytime from May through September—is lovely, resembling a perfect creation carved from wax then stamped with a red star at center. The flowers appear in bunches of twelve to fifteen individual blossoms. At one time the flowers were grown for buttonholes when that custom was a fashion statement for men. The custom did not last, because the flowers produce crystal beads of sweet nectar that is quite sticky.

Hoya carnosa 'Variegata' was introduced from Australia about 1802. The leaves are beautifully variegated with pale pink and cream shadings, making this plant worthy of being in a collection even if it never flowers.

Propagation is by cuttings.

The Passion Flower

There are over 350 members of the passion flower family, native to both the Old World and the New, but most are found in tropical America. Early in the 1600s, a Catholic friar, Emmanuele Villegas, while wandering through Mexico became the first recorded European to see the plant in bloom. In 1610 he presented a drawing of the blossom to the Roman theologian Giacomo Bosio, who immediately called it "the most extraordinary representation of the Cross Triumphant ever discovered in field or forest. The flower contains within

Rosary Vine
Ceropegia Woodii

itself not only the Savior's Cross but also the symbols of His Passion."

The flower described in the friar's drawing is most likely *Passiflora incarnata* (*passio* is passion and *floris*, flower), a native plant found in the southern United States and northern Mexico. It was called maypop or maracock by the Algonquin Indians, and was thought to relieve insomnia. The fruits are often used in jam.

Bosio was so excited by the admittedly stylized drawing that he wrote the following:

The filaments which surmount [the petals] resemble a fringe spattered with blood, thus seeming to represent the flail with which Christ was scourged. The column at which He was scourged rises from the center of the flower, the three nails with which He was nailed to the Cross are above it, and the column is surrounded by the Crown of Thorns. At the flower's exact center . . . there is a yellow zone bearing five blood-colored marks symbolic of the Five Wounds inflicted on Our Lord. The color of the column, the nails, and the crown is light green. Surrounding these elements is a kind of violet-colored nimbus composed of 72 filaments that correspond to the number of spines in the Crown of Thorns. The plant's numerous and attractive leaves are shaped like a lance-head, and remind us of the Lance of Longinus which pierced the Saviour's side. Their undersurface is marked with flecks of white which symbolized Judas' thirty pieces of silver.

Bosio forgot to note that the five petals and five sepals make up ten of the apostles—omitting Peter and Judas—that the sepals that remain on the vine after the flower falls represent the Trinity, and the whips of persecution can be seen in the coiling tendrils of the vine.

These flowers are truly exotic, resembling something usually found in a Victorian greenhouse. They are showstoppers when grown in the window or greenhouse or when spending a summer outdoors in the garden.

I have a *Passiflora* × *alatocaerulea* in a six-inch clay pot with an attached wire hanger that I set outside in the garden every summer, hanging it from an armillary sphere, so the vine grows up among the metal circles, flowering for most of the summer.

Among the plants available from nurseries are *Passiflora actinia*, with four-inch blooms of greenish white and a fringed corolla of lavender and white, blooming in the winter and bearing a sweet fragrance; *P.* × *alatocaerulea*, with large purple flowers and a delightful fragrance (the flowers are used in the manufacture of perfumes); *P. edulis*, with lavender flowers and edible fruit; *P.* 'Incense', bearing five-inch royal purple flowers with a corolla that entirely overlays the petals and has an intensely sweet perfume; and *P. vitifolia*, with red petals and sepals surrounding pure white filaments.

Temperatures should be above 55°F, though my plant has lived in the greenhouse, where 45°F is common. Fertilize every six weeks in summer, as too much feeding produces more leaves and fewer flowers. Use a soil mix of one-third each potting soil, peat moss, and sand. Passion flowers need plenty of sun, and keep the soil evenly moist during the growing season.

Flowers develop on the new growth, so prune the vine once a year while it is dormant, cutting back one-third of the canes and stopping just above a lateral bud.

Sow fresh seed in the spring. Germination takes about a month, and plants should flower in their second year.

Wax Plant ▶
Hoya carnosa

They can also be propagated from stem cuttings during the spring and summer months.

The Heart-Leaf Philodendron

Just because a plant is thought by many to be a cliché is no reason to ignore it, especially if it works. For example, there's a roadhouse outside of Tuxedo, New York, that all the buses and taxi-limos use for a rest stop, and the poor rider is forced to go inside whether wanting to or not. Some years ago, one of the owners brought in a heart-leaf philodendron and planted it in a dull corner where the illumination is provided by fluorescent lights in the ceiling high above. The vine began to climb, and he added strings. Now it stretches up the wall and across the ceiling of a giant room; at last visit, it was aiming for the woman at the cash register. Talk about a survivor.

Some years ago, I saw a similar treatment in a Manhattan apartment where the only light in the room was the reflection from an air-shaft window and two desk lamps. Yet a heart-leaf philodendron covered most of the ceiling, having been held with large staples that circled every third joint of the plant's stem.

The heart-leaf philodendron has been around since the late 1800s and through its entire history has been used for low-light situations where few other plants will grow. In the early 1930s the General Electric Company listed a number of plants that would do well away from the window with artificial light, and included in the list were the philodendrons. At one time this plant was more widely grown than any other houseplant in America.

These are jungle plants that begin life on dark, moist, spongy ground formed of layers and layers of vegetable debris. As they grow, they climb the nearest supports, striving to reach light that continually filters through the tree branches above. The ground serves only as a holdfast and short-term feeding post until the plants have sufficient anchorage to begin their climb.

While the plants are in the juvenile stage, the leaves are between four and six inches long, and on a mature plant up to twelve inches long, green on both the top and bottom.

The botanical name of this stalwart plant is *Philodendron scandens*. The genus is Greek for tree-loving, and *scandens* means to climb. It belongs to the subspecies *oxycardium*, this last meaning having a heart shape with a sharp point.

The stems produce aerial roots. If given a moist surface like a bark slab, a column of moss, or even a wood wall, they will cling tightly and eventually hold the plant aloft.

There are a number of cultivars, including *Philodendron scandens* var. *micans*, or the velvet-leaf philodendron, with bronzy red-violet leaves; *P. scandens* var. *miduhoi*, or jumbo velvet hearts, with larger leaves of a copper color; and *P. scandens* var. *aureum*, or the limeleaf vine, which has showy chartreuse leaves.

Soil should be one-third each of potting soil, peat moss, and sand, and this particular plant will do quite well growing in a jar of water. Temperatures should always be above 60°F, which explains why these vines do so well up at the ceiling. Although philodendrons will survive in areas with only 20 FC of light, the more light provided, the bigger the leaves. Heart-leaf philodendrons like to be misted on occasion.

Propagate with cuttings.

◀ Passion Flower
Passiflora × *alatocaerulea*

The Purple Bell Vine

The first mention I saw of the purple bell vine called it a miracle plant with an unbelievable number of beautiful flowers covering an attractive vine from head to foot. I took these words with a grain of salt, having read such pronouncements many times before, but I ordered seed and thought I'd give it a try. Was I surprised when the vine lived up to its press.

First registered in 1755, this fast-growing tropical beauty originally comes from Mexico. It's a perennial that will dependably bloom the first year; in fact, the earliest flowers appear about four months after seed germination. The botanical name is *Rhodochiton atrosanguineum*, with the genus meaning red cloak and the species referring to the color of a dark blood red. Older books often call it *R. volubile* (here the species means twining).

Masses of bell-shaped blossoms soon cover the vine, the flowers being the rich color of venous blood. The five-lobed inch-wide calyx is bell-shaped and a lighter shade of purple than the two-inch-long tubular corolla that flares out at the bottom into five lobes of unequal size. The leaves have long petioles and taper to a point from a heart-shaped base. A plant can climb about ten feet in a season, and the leaf and flower stalks will twine around a convenient support.

Many gardeners treat purple bells as half-hardy annuals, growing new plants every year, since they will dependably bloom four months from germination. Seeds will sprout in about fifteen days.

Use a soil mix of potting soil, humus, and sand, one-third each, and fertilize once a month during summer months. After a summer of bloom, the leaves on my plants begin to turn a deep purple, and growth ceases. But as they grow so easily from seed, this is never a major problem.

A Blooming Jasmine

A rose by any other name would smell as sweet, and so would any member of the Confederate jasmine family, no matter how confusing the terminology. The genus is *Trachelospermum*, which refers to the seed having a pronounced neck, a name derived from the Greek *trachelos*, or neck, and *sperma*, or seed.

My problem was with the species term of *mandianum*. No matter where I looked, I could find no reference to that particular name. Even *Hortus Third* missed it. Then just on a chance I looked in an old copy of *Hortus Second* (revised in 1941), where I found under *Trachelospermum jasminoides* a reference to a yellow-flowered form, listed as *Rhynchospermum Mandaianum*.

Today plants belonging to the *Rhynchospermum* are assigned either to *Chonemorpha* or back to *Trachelospermum*. *Chonemorpha* it isn't, since the flowers are decidedly pale yellow rather than white, and the leaves are shiny, not slightly hairy above or pubescent beneath. So it must be a *Trachelospermum*, but the jury is still out as to the veracity of the species name. The sap is white.

For the window garden, it's a beautiful vine with shiny green leaves and those fragrant light yellow flowers appearing throughout most of the year. This year my plant bloomed in April and May and then again in August.

The vine is a weaver, weaving itself back and forth and in and out as it climbs. You provide the warp, and the plant will become the woof (or, more properly, the weft).

Soil should be one-third each potting soil, peat moss, and sand. Allow the soil to dry slightly before watering again. Fertilize every two months except in winter.

Propagation is by cuttings.

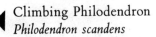

◀ Climbing Philodendron
Philodendron scandens

(following page)
Purple Bell Vine
Rhodochiton atrosanguineum ▶

PART FIVE

SUCCULENTS

Here are the plants for people worried about the responsibilities of watering, for the succulents will put up with a great deal of abuse when it comes to water requirements. But to me, their best qualities revolve around appearance, as their flowers are either beautiful, bizarre, or both, and the unusual leaf structures can make them look like visitors from another world.

Succulents and cactus are both xerophytes, or plants that have adapted to survival under conditions of a limited water supply. Both groups are called succulent because they have developed thick, fleshy stems or leaves designed to hold water. However, all cactuses belong in one family, the Cactaceae, and are the only plants that produce an areole, a special spot on the plants that generates spines. Therefore succulent is not a family name but applies to hundreds of different plants from all over the world. If a plant has the ability to store water in its leaves or stems, it's a succulent, regardless of what family it belongs to.

The Orchid or Pond-Lily Cactus

The orchid cactus is wisely named, for like orchids, the flowers of this unusual member of the cactus family are among the most beautiful found in nature. The genus *Epiphyllum* is from the Greek *epi*, upon, and *phyllos*, a leaf, as it was once thought that the flowers were borne on leaves, which are in reality flattened stems.

Although these plants are truly cactuses, they usually come from Brazil, Mexico, Costa Rica, and Guatemala, not deserts as one would suppose. These plants grow high up in the jungle canopy, where they find perfect drainage and receive enough nutrients to survive, brought to their roots by the action of tropical rains washing down the detritus caught in bark of trees. Their main branches are woody, with the green stems flat or thin with wavy margins. The typical cactus spines are missing on mature plants but are often present as bristles on seedlings or juvenile plants.

The older the plant, the more architectural it becomes, and the more blossoms that appear in early spring. Tiny buds appear between the scallops on the stems, buds that grow visibly larger every day until suddenly they open into truly breathtaking flowers, aglow with vibrant colors. The texture of the petals resembles that of glistening satin. Their glorious colors include white, yellow, red, scarlet, and red streaked with iridescent purple.

Among the many spectacular cultivars available are 'Argus', whose five-inch blossoms of apricot have a mandarin rose center and a yellow throat; 'Climax', with large off-white petals having central stripes of light lavender while the outer petals become a progressively darker amethyst that changes to red; 'Fireball', a seven- to nine-inch-wide flower of satiny orange with overtones of pink plus a yellow-green throat and pink anthers and pistil; and 'Morocco', a flower that combines light purple, red, yellow, medium purple, and cream, the outer two rows of petals becoming progressively darker and having yellow bases.

Orchid cactuses are adaptable plants. Temperatures can go as low as 40° during the dormancy of winter without causing damage, but freezing will kill. While direct sun in summer can burn the stems, plants will do well in filtered sun to bright shade. They should be watered well during active growth and during winter allowed to be dry, but when the stems begin to shrivel, water as fast as you can.

Perfect drainage is necessary, and I use one-third each potting soil, peat moss, and sand, and put the plants in hanging baskets lined with sphagnum moss. Fertilize once a month from April through September.

If possible, during the summer months, hang the cactuses outdoors under a tree or on the front porch. Mine summer under a sumac tree in the backyard. If the summer is unusually dry or the plants are sheltered from normal rains, you must water them, letting the soil dry out between applications.

Propagation is by rooted cuttings set in barely damp soil.

The Monster and the Golf-Ball

The *Euphorbias* or spurges comprise a collection of some of the oddest plants in the vegetable kingdom. Numbering over 1,600 species, they are herbs, shrubs, or trees that contain a milky juice, bloom with strange flowers, and in shape present to the world bizarre configurations unlike any

◀ Orchid Cactus
Epiphyllum × *hybridus*

other. The genus is named in honor of Euphorbus, a Greek physician to King Juba of Mauritania, an ancient district in Africa.

The milky sap is potentially dangerous in many species including the crown-of-thorns, *Euphorbia Milii*; snow-on-the-mountain, *E. marginata*; and the candelabra cactus, *E. lactea*. On the other hand, many people believe the Christmas poinsettia, *E. pulcherrima*, to be poisonous. However, though the sap can be an irritant to some susceptible persons, not one documented case involving a fatality has ever been reported. Native tribes in Africa often use this latex, which contains complex terpens, to poison arrow tips and to stupefy fish. *Hortus Third* suggests that many succulent euphorbias should not be planted along the edges of stocked pools, since exudates from broken roots might be fatal to the fish population.

The flowers are odd, too. In the poinsettia, for example, those bright red petals are really specialized leaves called bracts that masquerade as petals. The true flowers are the tiny yellow balls that cluster in the center of the bracts. If you look at them under a magnifying glass, you will see that some are pistillate, or female, and some are staminate, or male.

The two plants in my collection are what I call the monster and various references call the milk-barrel, *Euphorbia heptagona*, and *E. obesa*, a truly odd plant called the gingham golf-ball, the living-baseball, or the Turkish temple.

Euphorbia heptagona—with *heptagona* meaning seven angles, and referring to the ridges on the stem—comes from the Cape Province of South Africa. In the desert it becomes a thorny, erect succulent shrub about three feet high. The stem is about 1¾-inch thick, turning silvery brown with age and bearing tiny linear leaves and light brown spines. The light green leaves are found only on the top of the growing stem and are less than ¼ inch long, while the spines—really flower stems that never bear blossoms—are ¾ inch in length. The flowers, when they do appear, are small greenish yellow orbs that soon dry to brownish balls.

It's not much, but it's tough as nails and has been around the window garden for seven years.

The golf-ball bears the botanical name *Euphorbia obesa*, and obese it is. The "Turkish temple" moniker refers to the plant's onion-dome shape. The plants are small, spineless globes about five inches high and termed dioecious, since male and female flowers are on different plants, the males being somewhat pear-shaped and the females a bit rounder. The gray-green color is highlighted with rows of small knobs that resemble the stitching on a baseball, and additional markings on the surface call to mind the curving decorations on the Chrysler Building in Manhattan. The leaves, when they are in evidence, are so small as to be easily missed.

Propagation for the gingham golf-ball is limited to seed. Female plants must be pollinated from separate male plants, and the seed capsules must be covered with a small piece of netting to prevent loss of seed. Propagate the monster during the warm months of the year, using cuttings (but allow any wounds to dry) then using a sand-and-gravel mix in a warm place.

Both plants require perfect drainage, so use clay pots. Use a soil mix of potting soil, peat moss, and composted manure at one-third each and two-thirds in sand. Water only in the summer, letting the soil dry completely before watering again. The monster wants temperatures above 50°, and the golf-ball prefers at least 60°F. Both want sun, but the golf-ball prefers some shade from the noonday sun in summer.

Monster, Gingham Golf-Ball ▶
Euphorbia heptagona and *E. obesa*

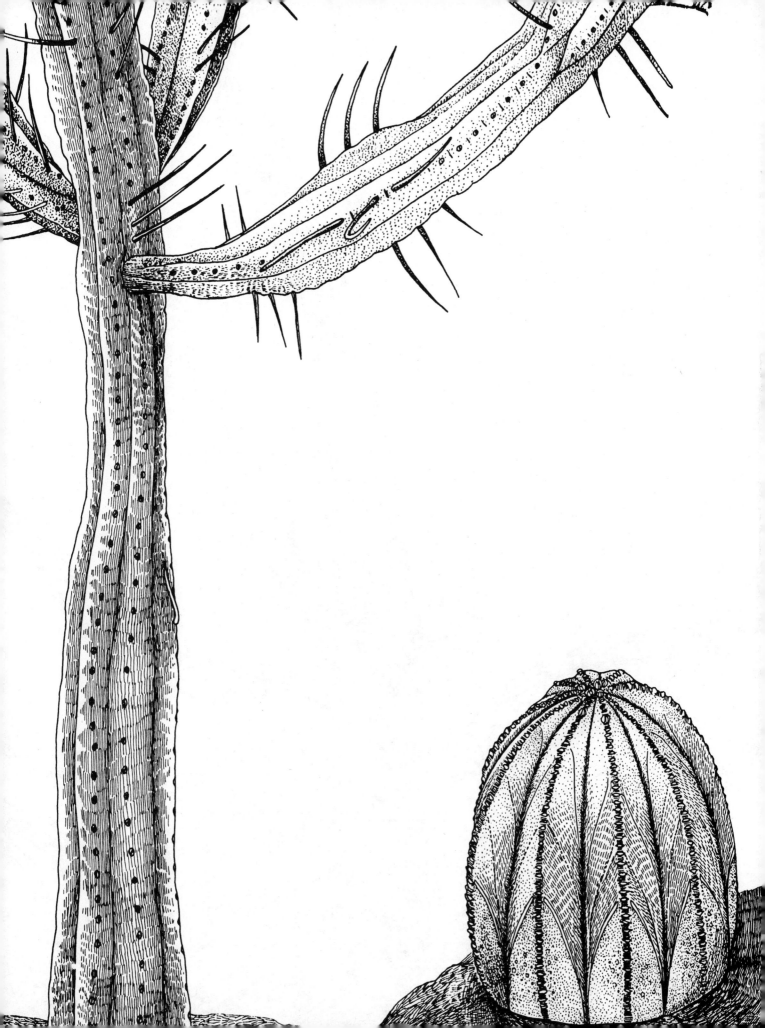

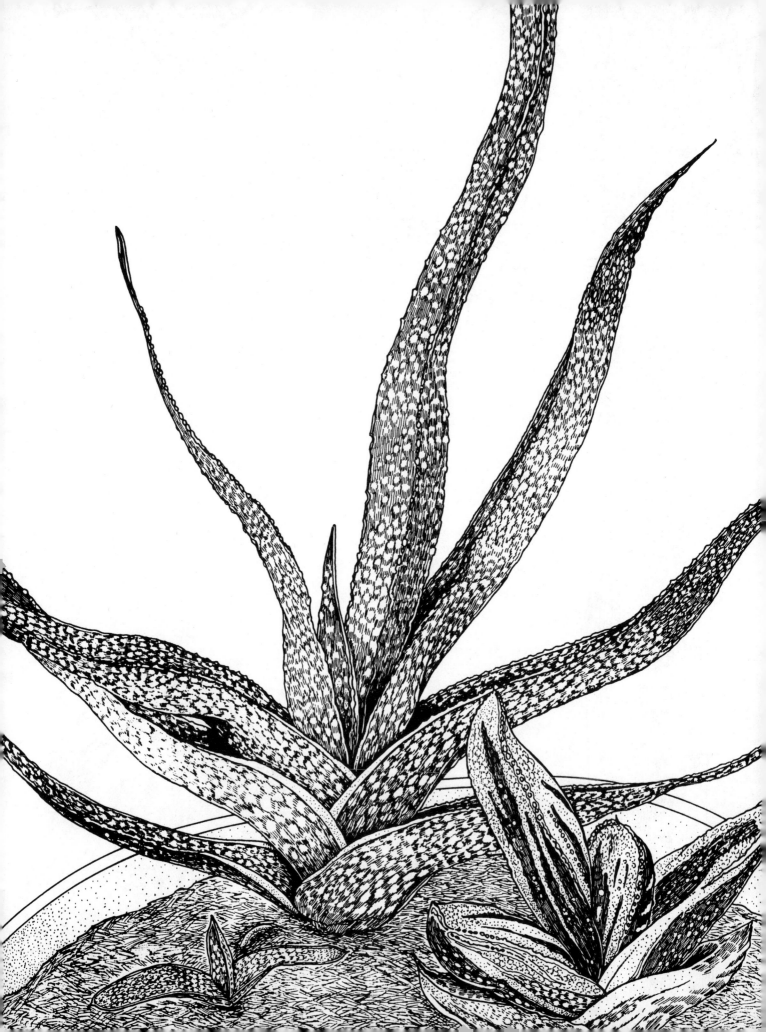

The Ox-Tongue Cactuses

Never having been licked by an ox's tongue, I can't be sure that this particular group of plants is properly named, but if such tongues look at all like I imagine them to be, most of these plants are right on. All except one of the common names in current use revolves around the tongue and include cow-tongue cactus, lawyer's-tongue, mother-in-law's tongue, and, strangely, Dutch-wings. The genus is *Gasteria* and is named for the Latin *gaster*, or belly, referring to the swollen base of the flower tube. There are some fifty species of these succulents, all from South Africa. They are closely allied to the aloes but are easily recognized because of the flower form. They are not cactuses but actually members of the lily family.

The long, fleshy, but tough leaves grow in ranks of two, or some slowly spiral, eventually becoming rosettes. The leaves do resemble animal tongues, even including the raised specks or tubercles that often cover the surface, much like taste buds. Some twenty species or cultivars are available from nurseries and would make a fine theme for a collection of unusual plants.

Gasterias are also excellent plants for people on the go, since the thick leaves point to their ability to survive up to a month without water. However, for healthy growth, they should be watered well during the summer months, then kept almost waterless during the winter dormant period. Temperatures should be kept above 50°F. Keep strong sun to a minimum, as too much causes the leaves to turn brown and lose much of their character—partial shade is best. A good soil mix is one-quarter each of potting soil, composted manure, peat moss, and sand. Fertilize these plants once in spring, summer, and fall.

A number of these plants are lumped under the name of *Gasteria maculata*, where *maculata* means spotted. The leaves of these plants can grow to a length of eight inches and about an inch wide, attractively speckled with raised off-white oval spots in an abstract pattern. Flowers are pink, ¾ inch long, and bloom on scapes up to three feet high.

For those with limited space, look for *Gasteria nigricans marmorata* 'Variegata', a charming plant with fat and short leaves—less than an inch long—growing like little bow ties, each marked with dark brown and ivory stripes, or *Gasteria* 'Silver Stripes', a slightly larger hybrid that bears pebbles in green stripes on a gray-green background.

Propagation is by offsets. If they have few or no roots, they should be allowed to dry before being potted.

The Drunkard's-Dream

The drunkard's-dream or dancing-bones cactus is one of five species of cactuses originally found in Brazil. First described in 1834, the genus is *Hatiora*, and is an anagram for Thomas Hariot, a botanist of the sixteenth century. The species is *salicornioides*, meaning like a *Salicornia*, these being a small genus of plants found near the ocean that have thick-jointed leafless stems and are commonly called glassworts.

The jointed stems are tan to green and strongly resemble small bottles, with smaller bottles growing from what would be the caps. Under strong light, tiny purple spots appear along the stems with no regular pattern. The typical cactus spines are reduced to minute patches of fuzz at the bottle-cap position. Growing plants also resemble the stylistic skeletons and bones

Ox-Tongues
Gasteria maculata; *G. nigricans marmorata*
'Variegata' and 'Silver Stripes'

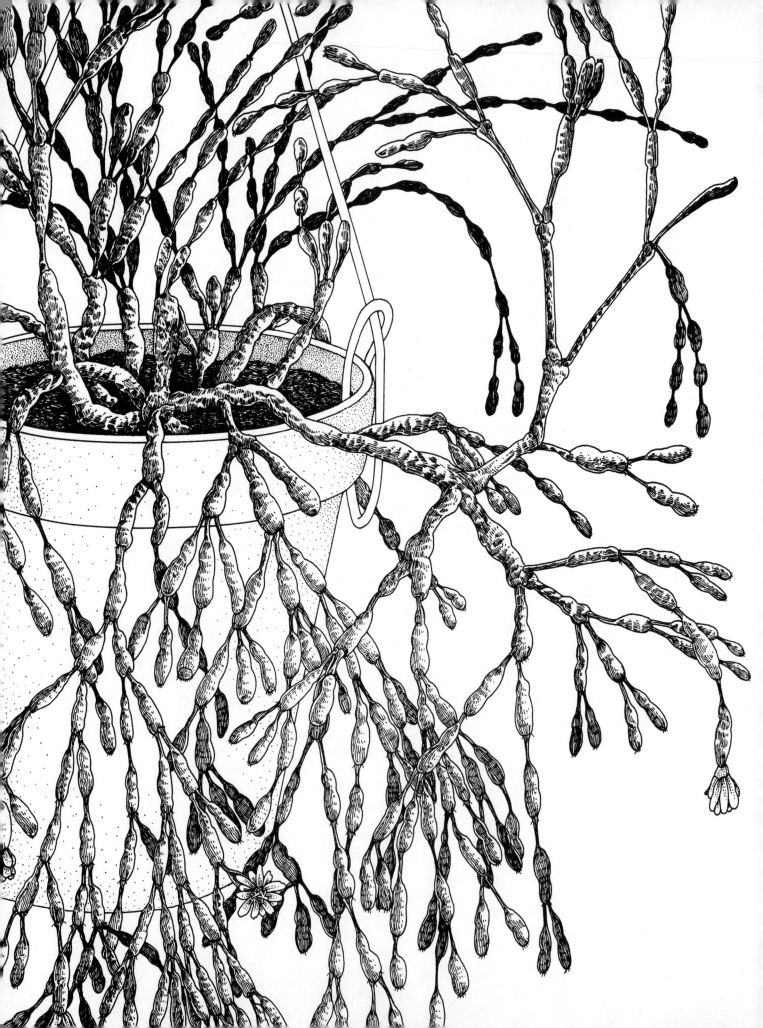

found on confections featured in many religious holidays in Central and South America.

Waxy yellow flowers open only in sunlight and are wheel-shaped when completely open. They fade to an orange-salmon color. In the United States, plants bloom from January to March but occasionally as late as April. The plant is supposed to set fruit: a small, white, translucent berry. I've never seen any.

Hatioras are epiphytes, or plants that use trees or other plants merely as a support without being parasitic. In 1915, while collecting in Rio de Janeiro, Dr. J. N. Rose wrote, "The plant grows on trunks of trees, its roots long and fibrous, [16 inches] long or more and wrapped about the trunk of the tree; at first [the plant] is erect, then spreading, and finally pendent."

Since hatioras come from the Brazilian jungles, temperatures should always be above 60°F. The best soil mix offers perfect drainage, so use potting soil, peat moss, and composted manure at one-third each, and two-thirds of sand. Under the best of conditions, this soil mix should be kept evenly moist, which means watering as often as you can. It sounds like a conflict in terminology, but remember where these plants grow. My plant spends the summer hanging under the sumac tree in the garden. I fertilize once a month from April to September.

Propagate by cuttings in spring.

The Pearly Moonstones

Over the years, most of the plants in my various window gardens have been potted in old-fashioned clay pots, many of them picked up at garage sales and the rest at end-of-the-year sales at nursery and garden centers. A few are in open-wire hanging baskets. Unless they are in self-watering pots of a very plain design, none are in plastic. In addition, I have a large collection of turn-of-the-century jardinieres that pots can sit within for a special show or display either at the table or out on the terrace.

There is, however, one exception. The plant known as pearly moonstones sits in a six-sided Chinese porcelain pot decorated with deep blue stylized birds and flowers, sitting on a saucer with a light blue rim. The leaves of this plant so resemble carved jade that a pot of any less elegance would never do.

Moonstones belong to the genus *Pachyphytum*, meaning a thick plant and referring to the heavy stems and globular leaves of these succulents. The species is *oviferum* because the leaves are egglike. They belong to the same family as the time-honored jade plant.

Originally from Mexico, plants rarely reach above six inches. Half-inch stems that bear the scars of old and abandoned leaves end in a cluster of tightly packed leaves, which are termed glaucous because they are covered with pale gray-blue powder that is easily rubbed off. In the bright light of summer, the leaf color intensifies, and the leaf surface glows with pink highlights. Older leaves eventually shrivel and fall off. When a stem bends over the soil, it also gives rise to aerial roots.

Eventually, when the stems become too tall and naked, it is time to start new plants—easily accomplished by cutting off the stems some two inches below the leaves and rooting the shorter piece. Individual leaves also will root.

For the best color, give plants all the sun you can. Temperatures should always be above 50°F. The best soil mix is potting soil, peat moss, and composted manure, at one-third each, and two-thirds sand. Water only when the soil is dry, and let plants rest in the winter months, watering only if the leaves show signs of shriveling.

Drunkard's-Dream
Hatiora salicornioides

The Sansevierias

For years I thought that the name *sansevieria* meant 'without evieria.' I never bothered to look up evieria, assuming it to be a rare or underused botanical term referring to seed structure or something of that ilk, knowing that one day I'd take the time to track the meaning down and straighten it out in my mind. Well, much to my chagrin, I just checked the *Dictionary of Gardening* and found that the name *sansevieria* is in honor of Raimond de Sansgrio, the Prince of Sanseviero (1710–1771). As to the reason for honoring the prince in this manner, I can find no reference.

Often called bowstring hemp—because the tough fibers that make up the leathery leaves have been used for bowstrings, and also for making hats, mats, and rope—the other common names are Devil's-tongue, good-luck plant, hemp plant, and, to a few who have trouble with their spouse's mother, mother-in-law's tongue, a reference no doubt to the thick, flat, and pointed leaves found on most of the genus.

These stalwart plants are members of the lily family, a fact that is not at all in evidence until they bloom. Then the plants produce spidery night-blooming flowers, each with six pale green petals and long curving stamens, and exude a penetrating but sweet fragrance that quickly fills the room. Where the flower base meets the stem, they drip with crystal beads of sugary nectar with a sharp undertaste.

Over seventy species and cultivars are now available and include leaves that are spear-shaped and either straight or with fluted edges; banded with various whites, silvers, endless greens, numerous yellows, or buff-colored blotches; and ranging in size from the very small to the very tall.

The most common species is *Sansevieria trifasciata*, usually called the snake plant, which is often found growing in the windows of Mexican restaurants and Chinese launderers, where the combination of steam and heat pushes them on to great spurts of growth. In fact, the leaves often reach a length that borders on four feet. Flowering can occur at almost any time.

Of the three that I grow in our window, the strangest is *Sansevieria cylindrica patula*, an oddball plant with cylindrically curved and solid stems of dark green with darker bands that verge on black. As they grow, they assume the shape of a fan.

The cutest is *Sansevieria trifasciata* 'Golden Hahnii', or the gilt-edged bird's-nest, an East Indian clone that bears cup-shaped leaves dashed with wide, creamy yellow bands. And for added color, there is *Sansevieria trifasciata* 'Laurentii', with yellow bands on a dark green background, originally found growing in the wilds of Zaire.

Sansevierias are tender plants. They cannot take temperatures much below 50°F for any length of time, preferring instead days and nights between 60° and 70°F.

As to light requirements, many people think that these succulent-like plants will do well in dark corners, but except for a few cultivars like 'Nelsonii'—a slow-growing plant with dark green leaves that is specifically listed for room corners with poor light—most need full sun or at best partial shade that offers diffused sunlight.

Use a soil mix of one-third potting soil, one-third peat moss, and one-third sharp sand, adding to each gallon of the mix a teaspoon of superphosphate, a dash of ground limestone, and two teaspoons of 5-10-5 fertilizer. From early spring to late fall, allow the soil to dry between watering, and during the same time period, fertilize every three months. But remember in winter to use just enough water to keep the leaves from shriveling, and never add plant food. Too much water under chilly

Pearly Moonstones
Pachyphytum oviferum ▶

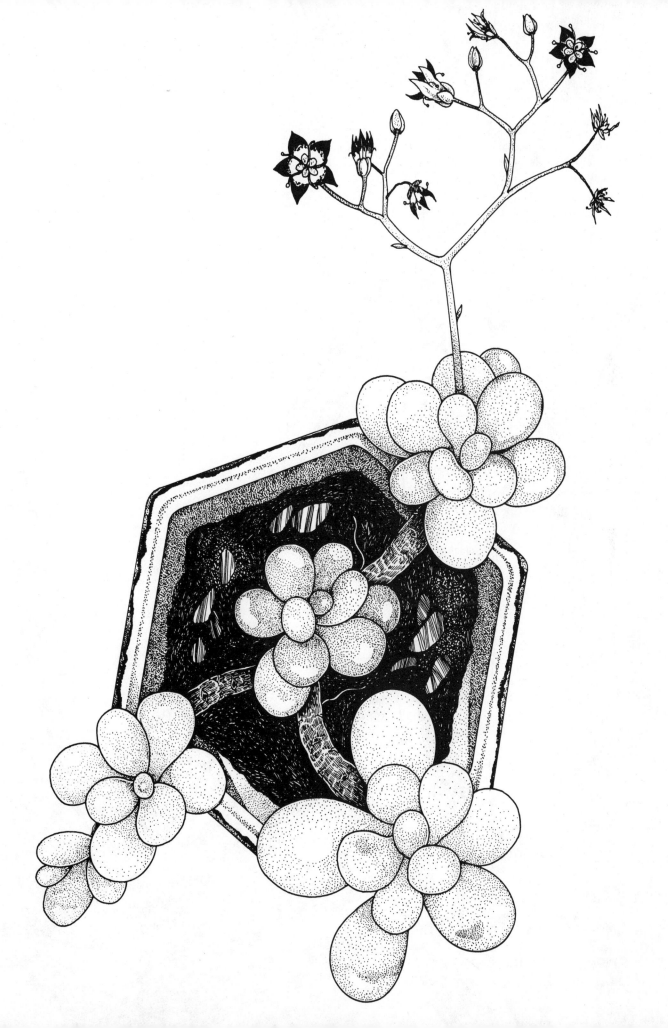

temperatures with limited winter light will soon spell death for these plants. They do well when potbound, so you need not bother with repotting except every three years or so.

Propagate by dividing the plants any time of the year except in a northern winter and also by leaf cuttings rooted in sand, using bottom heat. Don't use the cutting method for 'Laurentii', as the new plants will lose the yellow strips and revert back to the species.

The Stapelias

An orange sun forms one fiery bubble in a flat and deep blue sky. The only signs of movement on the vast horizon are the shimmering waves of heat as they rise in frantic whorls from the sea of sand that seems to stretch on forever. And it is hot—dry and hot.

At first glance, all seems to be lifeless and bare: just the sand and stone enveloped in a deathly stillness. Then in the shady crook of a large rock, I see a twisted bunch of thick, green, tapered stems all splotched with purple, and I hear the buzz of a lone fly. I look again and see a vivid orange-and-purple flower. Flower? What kind of flower looks more like tooled and wrinkled leather tattooed with strange colors rather than the jewel-line tones of a normal floral display? And the fly; why the fly? And, too, the smell—ever so slight—of spoiled fruit or a bit of meat past its prime.

Suddenly I see the fly walk across a petal, crisscrossing the thickened ring that stands slightly above and to the center of the pleated petals, disappearing over the ring's edge, down into a dark crevasse, where it buzzes all the louder, like a bee with honey.

Then the buzzing stops, and the fly

appears again. Only now a bright yellow ball of pollen is stuck to one leg. It shakes the leg trying to dislodge the added load, thinks better of it, and spirals up and around, descending to another nearby flower. And what I've witnessed is the pollination of a blossom by a fly in a meadow of sand. For the desert is too hot and barren for a honeybee and too dry and dusty for the typical flower of the field.

Although the stems of the stapelias—and stems they are, for the leaves are minuscule—have never been the hit of the houseplant world, the flowers certainly have. Bizarre, unique, and indelicate, they always elicit response when displayed at flower shows, generating choruses of ohs and ahs when plants accompany me on a lecture.

"I'd call it a crochet flower," said one lady. "They don't look real, more a creation of hook and needle, I'd say."

"Rather a strange hook and needle," said her husband and quietly added, "It doesn't smell that good either."

The genus, *Stapelia*, is named after Johannes Bodaeus van Stapel, a physician of Amsterdam who died in 1631. And there are hundreds of species belonging to a number of genera. The most successful that I've grown are the time-honored *Stapelia variegata*, or spotted toad flower; *S. longipes*; *S. cylista*; *S. nobilis*; *S. pasadenensis*; and *Edithcolea grandis*. *S. pasadenensis* can produce a flower over six inches in diameter that, unlike the other flowers, is best kept outdoors when in bloom, since it can smell a lot like living near a large landfill.

Stapelias are succulents, so the primary rule of care is to provide adequate drainage. I use a potting mix of one-third standard potting soil, one-third composted manure, and one-third sharp sand, with a liberal sprinkling of small charcoal chips and some bird gravel. I fertilize only every few weeks in the hottest part of the summer.

Snake Plants
Sansevieria trifasciata; *S. cylindrica patula*; and *S. trifasciata* 'Golden Hahnii'

While most stapelias will endure a temperature of 40°F, they do not respond with favor to such a chilly atmosphere. And if allowed to sit in even damp soil when the temperature falls that low, they will usually begin to rot. I withhold water from November to March, moving the plants to my study, where the temperatures fluctuate between 50° and 70°F.

Take cuttings of your plants in the late spring when the weather is on the warm side. The cutting is best removed from the joint of a parent stem then set aside for a few days until the cut or break is dry. Use pieces at least an inch long.

Push cuttings into a dish or pot of warm, moist, and clean sand to a depth of half to one inch. Roots will begin to appear in a few days.

Seeds should be sown when fresh, and any of the commercial "sow and grow" mixes can be used, but place the containers on heating cables. When seedlings appear, provide adequate ventilation and shade from the hot sun. In about three months, the seedlings can be moved to three-inch pots.

The only serious pest I've ever encountered with these plants is the mealybug. To eliminate this beast, touch cotton swabs dipped in alcohol directly to the insect's body. For severe infestations, sterilize the soil, and wash stems and roots in denatured alcohol for a few minutes, then rinse in warm water before replanting.

Stapelias or Carrion Flowers
◀ *Stapelia longipes*; *S. cylista*; *Edithcolea grandis*; *S. variegata*; *S. nobilis*

PART SIX

APPENDIXES

Appendix A:
Sources of Supply

The following suppliers grow and sell seeds or live plants for shipment throughout the United States and Canada. You phone or order by mail, and they will ship by United Parcel Service. Over the years, I've ordered hundreds of plants, and almost everything has arrived in fine condition. When it has not, the nurseries have rectified the mistake.

The Banana Tree. 715 Northampton Street, Easton, Pennsylvania 18042. Tropical seeds and bulbs, many of them exotic. Catalog is $1.00.

Chiltern Seeds. Bortree Stile, Ulverston, Cumbria LA12 7PB, England. A marvelous catalog with seeds from all over the world. Send an airmail letter for current price of catalog.

Endangered Species. Box 1830, Tustin, California 92681. Bamboos, grasses, hoyas, New Zealand flax, euphorbias, sansevierias, and other unusual plants. Catalog is $5.00.

Glasshouse Works. Church Street, P.O. Box 97, Stewart, Ohio 45778. A fascinating collection of houseplants, including the rare and unusual. Hoyas, aglaonemas, and many, many more. Catalog is $1.50.

Greenlife Gardens. 101 County Line Road, Griffin, Georgia 30223. A large collection of orchid cactus cultivars and other epiphytic cactuses. Catalog is $2.00.

J. L. Hudson, Seedsmen. P.O. Box 1058, Redwood City, California 94064. A fascinating catalog full of unusual plant seeds from around the world.

K&L Cactus Nursery. 2712 Stockton Boulevard, Galt, California 95652. A large selection of cactus and succulents. Catalog is $2.00.

Karutz Greenhouses. 1408 Sunset Drive, Vista, California 92083. Begonias, vines, and many other tropical plants. Catalog is $2.00.

Lauray of Salisbury. Undermountain Road, Salisbury, Connecticut 06068. Begonias and many other exotic tropicals. Catalog is $2.00.

Logee's Greenhouses. Danielson, Connecticut 06239. One of the oldest and best sources of houseplants in the country. Many, many begonias and other tropical plants. Catalog is $3.00.

Park Seed Company. Greenwood, South Carolina 29647. One of the oldest seed houses in America and home to a large selection of flower seeds for indoor gardens. Catalog is free.

The Plant Kingdom. Box 7273, Lincoln Acres, California 92047. A very large selection of unusual plants, including twenty-three species and cultivars of the passion flower. Catalog is $1.00.

Scotty's Desert Plants. 11588 South Academy Avenue, Selma, California 93662. The inheritors of Altman's Specialty Plants, they carry many unusual and attractive succulents. Catalog is $1.00.

Singer's Growing Things. 17806 Plummer Street, Northridge, California 91325. A large selection of succulent plants. Catalog is $1.00.

Stallings Exotic Nursery. 910 Encinitas Boulevard, Encinitas, California 92024. Many exotic tropicals, including unusual grasses and vines. Catalog is $2.00.

Thompson & Morgan. P.O. Box 100, Farmingdale, New Jersey 08527. One of England's oldest seed houses, now with offices in America. They have many houseplant seeds. Catalog is free.

The following companies offer supplies for your window garden or greenhouse:

Charley's Greenhouse Supplies. 1569 Memorial Highway, Mount Vernon, Washington 98257. A major supplier of greenhouse-related items, including brackets for hanging pots. Catalog is $2.00.

Florist Products, Inc. 2242 North Palmer Drive, Schaumburg, Illinois 60173. Tools, fertilizers, and greenhouse equipment.

Mellinger's Inc. 2310 West South Range Road, North Lima, Ohio 44452. They sell plants, but their true forte is in the vast number of greenhouse and houseplant supplies they carry. Catalog is free.

Walt Nicke Company. 36 McLeod Lane, P.O. Box 433, Topsfield, Massachusetts 01983. The first of the mail-order suppliers of houseplant and greenhouse items, and now a veritable supermarket of supplies. Catalog is 50¢.

Appendix B: Plant Societies

American Bamboo Society. 1101 San Leon, Solana Beach, California 92075.

American Begonia Society. P.O. Box 502, Encinitas, California 92024.

American Plant Life Society. P.O.Box 150, La Jolla, California 92038.

Cactus and Succulent Society. 2631 Fairgreen Avenue, Arcadia, California 91006.

Friends of the Fig. 840 Ralph Road, Conyers, Georgia 30208.

Hoya Society International. P.O. Box 54271, Atlanta, Georgia 30308.

Indoor Citrus & Rare Fruit Society. 176 Coronado Avenue, Los Altos, California 94022.

Indoor Light Gardening Society of America. 128 West 58th Street, New York, New York 10019.

International Aroid Society, Inc. P.O. Box 43–1853, South Miami, Florida 33143.

International Asclepiad Society. 10 Moorside Terrace, Drighlington, BD11 1HX, England.

International Cactus and Succulent Society. P.O. Box 253, Odessa, Texas 79760.

Appendix C: Best Ways to Reproduce 179 Different Houseplants

(W = root in water)

Achimenes (*Achimenes* spp.) Seeds; scales rubbed from tubers, sown as seeds; shoot cuttings in spring; leaf petiole cutting.

Aeonium (*Aeonium* spp.) Seeds; leaf cuttings; division.

African evergreen (*Syngonium podophyllum*) Stem cuttings. (W)

African milkbush (*Euphorbia Tirucalli*) Stem cuttings, but air-dry wound first.

African violet (*Saintpaulia* spp.) Seeds; leaf petiole cutting; division. (W)

Aloe (*Aloe* spp.) Suckers; top cuttings.

Aluminum plant (*Pilea Cadierei*) Cuttings.

Amaryllis (*Hippeastrum* 'Leopoldii Hybrid') Seeds, but will not always breed true; bulblets.

Amazon lily (*Eucharis grandiflora*) Seeds; bulblets.

Anthurium (*Anthurium* spp.) Fresh seed with bottom heat 80°F (26.5°C); top cuttings; division when repotting.

Artillery plant (*Pilea Microphylla*) Cuttings.

Asparagus fern (*Asparagus* spp.) Seeds; division when repotting.

Aurora borealis plant (*Kalanchoe Fedtschenkoi* 'Marginata') Stem cuttings, but water sparingly.

Avocado (*Persea americana*) Seeds; stem cuttings in spring. (W)

Azalea (*Rhododendron* × *hybridia*) Top cuttings from new growth.

Banana (*Musa nana*) Seeds, but may take a year to sprout; suckers.

Begonia (*Begonia* spp.):
   a) Fibrous-rooted or bedding begonias by seeds; stem cuttings; division. (W)
   b) Cane-stemmed begonias by stem cuttings.
   c) Rhizomatious begonias by division of rhizome, including an "eye" in each section; tip cuttings.
   d) Rex begonias by seeds; tip cuttings; leaf-section cuttings.
   e) Tuberous-rooted begonias by seeds; division of tuber with "eye" in each section.

Bird-of-paradise (*Strelitzia reginae*) Seeds; division of new shoots.

Black-eyed Susan vine (*Thunbergia alata*) Seeds; cuttings.

Bloodleaf (*Iresine Herbstii*) Cuttings. (W)

Blood lily (*Haemanthus*) Bulblets.

Blue marguerite (*Felicia amelloides*) Seeds; cuttings; division.

Bottlebrush (*Callistemon lanceolatus*) Seeds; stem cuttings of ripened wood.

Bougainvillea (*Bougainvillea* spp.) Seeds; stem cuttings from ripened wood.

Brazilian-firecracker (*Manettia inflata*) Stem cuttings.

Browallia (*Browallia speciosa*) Seeds; cuttings.

Caladium (*Caladium* spp.) Divide tubers in spring with bottom heat of 70°F (21°C).

Calathea (*Calathea* spp.) Division in spring.

Calico plant (*Alternanthera ficoides*) Cuttings in spring; division.

Camellia (*Camellia* spp.) Tip cuttings in fall with rooting hormone.

Campanula (*Campanula isophylla*) Cuttings.

Carrion flower (*Stapelia* spp.) Seeds; cuttings; division.

Cast-iron plant (*Aspidistra elatior*) Division.

Cattleya orchid (*Cattleya* spp.) Division with at least four pseudobulbs to a plant.

Century plant (*Agave* spp.) Seeds; suckers.

Cherry tomato (*Lycopersicum* var. *cerasiferme* 'Tiny Tim') Seeds from your own fruit.

Chinese evergreen (*Aglaonema modestum*)
Seeds; division of mature plant; joint
cuttings.

Christmas cactus (*Schlumbergera Bridgesii*)
Leaf joint.

Christmas-kalanchoe (*Kalanchoe Blossfeldiana*)
Seeds; stem cuttings.

Cigar flower (*Cuphea ignea*) Seeds, but needs
light to germinate; cuttings.

Cissus (*Cissus* spp.) Cuttings with a piece of
the older branch. (W)

Citrus (*Citrus* spp.) Seeds, but not always
true to type; cuttings in spring.

Clerodendrum (*Clerodendrum* spp.) Tip
cuttings.

Cobra lily (*Darlingtonia californica*) Seeds;
division of mature plants.

Coffee (*Coffea arabica*) Seeds; firm cuttings
with bottom heat of 80°F (26.5°C).

Coleus (*Coleus* spp.) Seeds; cuttings. (W)

Columnea (*Columnea* spp.) Tip cuttings;
division; single leaves will eventually
root, but it takes forever.

Coral-bead plant (*Nertera granadensis*) Seeds;
division.

Coral vine (*Antigonon leptopus*) Seeds;
cuttings.

Crotons (*Codiaeum* var. *pictum*) Seeds, but
never true to type; tip cuttings.

Crown-of-thorns (*Euphorbia Milii*) Stem
cuttings, but allow wound to heal first.

Cyclamen (*Cyclamen* spp.) Seeds sown at
65°F (18°C) and, when germinated,
grown at 55°F (13°C); tuber cuttings.

Devil's ivy (*Epipremnum aureum*) Tip
cuttings.

Dracaena (*Dracaena* spp.) Cuttings; stem
sections; air layer. (W)

Drunkard's-dream (*Hatiora salicornioides*)
Stem cuttings of joints.

Dumb (*Diffenbachia* spp.) Stem sections;
suckers; air layer. (W)

Echeveria (*Echeveria* spp.) Cuttings; leaf
cuttings; offshoots.

Egyptian star cluster (*Pentas lanceolata*)
Seeds; softwood cuttings in spring.

English daisy (*Bellis perennis*) Seeds; division.

English ivy (*Hedera Helix*) Cuttings. (W)

Exacum (*Exacum affine*) Seeds; cuttings.

False aralia (*Dizygotheca elegantissima*) Seeds;
air layer.

Fern, Boston (*Nephrolepis exaltata*) Rooting
buds on runners; division.

Fern, blue (*Polypodium aureum*
'Mandaianum') Break off a large, hairy
"foot" and pot separately.

Fern, mother (*Asplenium bulbiferum*) Tiny
plantlets develop on front tops, to be
potted.

Fern, rabbit's foot (*Davallia fejeensis*) Break
off a "foot" and repot.

Fern, staghorn (*Platycerium* spp.) Tiny
"pups" at root tips may be potted.

Fig, creeping (*Ficus pumila*) Stem cuttings.

Fig, fiddle-leaf (*Ficus lyrata*) Air layer.

Fig, fruit (*Ficus carica*) Hardwood cuttings.

Firecracker plant (*Cuphea ignea*) Seeds; leaf
cuttings in summer; stem cuttings.

Flamebush (*Calliandra emarginata*) Seeds; new
stem cuttings.

Flame violet (*Episcia cupreata*) Seeds;
cuttings; rosettes from runners.

Flamingo flower (*Anthurium scherzeranum*)
Stem cuttings.

Flowering maple (*Abutilon* × *hybridia*)
Seeds; stem cuttings from new growth
in spring.

Forest lily (*Veltheimia viridifolia*) Bulblets;
single, whole leaf stuck upright in
medium will produce bulblets around
base.

Freesia (*Freesia* × *hybridia*) Cormlets.

Fuchsia (*Fuchsia* × *hybridia*) Seeds; stem
cuttings in spring.

Garden nasturtium (*Tropaeolum majus*) Seeds;
cuttings.

Gardenia (*Gardenia* spp.) Half-hard cuttings from new growth with bottom heat of 75°F (24°C).

Gas plant (*Dictamnus albus*) Seeds; root cuttings; division.

Gazania (*Gazania rigens*) Seeds; cuttings; division.

Geranium (*Pelargonium* spp.) Stem cuttings.

German ivy (*Senecio mikanioides*) Stem cuttings. (W)

Gill-over-the-ground (*Glechoma hederacea*) Cuttings.

Glory lily (*Gloriosa Rothschildiana*) Seeds; cut tuber including an "eye," dusting cut end with powdered charcoal.

Gloxinia (*Sinningia* spp.) Seeds; sprouts; leaf cuttings; division of tuber with "eye."

Golden-trumpet (*Allamanda cathartica Hendersonii*) Softwood cuttings in spring.

Good-luck leaf (*Kalanchoe pinnata*) Tiny plantlets fall to earth and grow.

Green marble vine (*Senecio Herreianus*) Division; cuttings.

Guinea goldvine (*Hibbertia volubilis*) Stem cuttings.

Hardy chinese orchid (*Bletilla striata*) Division during dormant period.

Heliotrope (*Heliotropium arborescens*) Seeds; stem cuttings.

Hibiscus (*Hibiscus Rosa-sinensis*) Stem cuttings of firm young shoots in spring with bottom heat of 70°F (21°C).

Hoya (*Hoya* spp.) Stem cuttings of previous year's growth in spring with bottom heat of 75°F (23°C).

Hydrangea (*Hydrangea macrophylla*) Cuttings of young shoots with at least three nodes in spring.

Impatiens (*Impatiens* spp.) Seeds; cuttings. (W)

Inch plant, also called wandering Jew (*Trandescantia* spp.) Cuttings. (W)

Jade plant (*Crassula* spp.) Stem cuttings; leaf cuttings. (W)

Japanese aralia (*Fatsia japonica*) Seeds; stem cuttings; air layer.

Jerusalem cherry (*Solanum Pseudocapsicum*) Seeds; stem cuttings.

Jungle-flame (*Ixora coccinea*) Firm stem cuttings in spring at bottom heat of 85°F (29°C).

Kaffir lily (*Clivia miniata* 'Grandiflora') Seeds; division when repotting.

Kenilworth ivy (*Cymbalaria muralis*) Seeds; cuttings. (W)

Lantana (*Lantana Camara*) Seeds; softwood cuttings.

Leopard plant (*Ligularia tussilaginea*) Division when repotting.

Lily (*Lilium* spp.) Seeds; bulblets; bulbils that appear at leaf axils; individual scales from mother bulb laid flat on sphagnum moss.

Lily-of-the-Nile (*Agapanthus africanus*) Seeds; division in spring when repotting.

Lipstick plant (*Aeschynanthus Lobbianus*) Stem cuttings.

Lobster-law (*Heliconia humilis*) Seeds; division.

Miracle leaf (*Kalanchoe pinnata*) Plantlets formed in leaf notches may be potted.

Monkey flower (*Mimulus aurantiacus*) Seeds; stem cuttings.

Monstera (*Monstera deliciosa*) Seeds; stem sections; stem cuttings. (W)

Moonflower (*Ipomoea alba*) Seeds, but notch the seed coat to hasten germination; stem cuttings, but chancey.

Moses-in-the-cradle (*Rhoeo spathacea*) Seeds; suckers.

Natal plum (*Carissa grandiflora*) Seeds; stem cuttings.

Nerve plant (*Fittonia Vereschaffeltii*) Stem cuttings with bottom heat 75°F (23°C).

Night-blooming cereus (*Selenicereus* spp.) Joint or tip cuttings.

Norfolk Island pine (*Araucaria heterophylla*) Seeds; six-inch tip cuttings from terminal shoots.

Norse fire plant (*Columnea* × 'Stavanger') Division; stem cuttings.

Oleander (*Nerium Oleander*) Stem cuttings. (W)

Orchid cactus (*Epiphyllum* spp.) Cuttings of mature shoots in spring.

Oxalis (*Oxalis* spp.) Seeds; offsets when repotting.

Palms (all varieties) Fresh seeds with bottom heat of 70°F (21°C); suckers.

Panda plant (*Kalanchoe tomentosa*) Stem cuttings; individual leaves on moist sand.

Parachute plant (*Ceropegia Sandersonii*) Joint cuttings.

Passionflower (*Passiflora* spp.) Seeds; stem cuttings.

Peperomia (*Peperomia* spp.) Soft wood cuttings; division.

Petunia (*Petunia* × hybridia) Seeds; cuttings.

Philodendron (*Philodendron* spp.) Seeds; tip cuttings; air layer; stem sections with several leaves. (W)

Piggyback plant (*Tolmiea Menziesii*) Leaf petiole cuttings. (W)

Pineapple lily (*Eucomis comosa*) Bulblets.

Pitcher plant (*Sarracenia* spp.) Seeds; division in early spring.

Plover-eggs (*Adromischus Cooperi*) Stem cuttings; individual leaves on moist sand.

Plumbago (*Plumbago capensis*) Tip cuttings; root cuttings; division when repotting.

Pocketbook plant (*Calceolaria* spp.) Seeds; stem cuttings.

Poinsettia (*Euphorbia pulcherrima*) Soft or hardwood cuttings allowing the wound to heal.

Prayer plant (*Maranta leuconeura*) Division when repotting.

Quilted-taffeta plant (*Hoffmannia refulgens*) Stem cuttings.

Resurrection plant (*Selaginella lepidophylla*) Pin a frond tip to damp sand or peat moss, and new plant will form.

Rochea coccinea Stem cuttings, air-dried for a few days in spring or summer.

Rouge plant (*Rivina humilis*) Seeds; stem cuttings.

Rubber plant (*Ficus elastica*) Seeds; air layer.

Sacred Bo-tree (*Ficus religiosa*) Seeds; air layer.

Scarborough lily (*Vallota speciosa*) Seeds; bulblets.

Screw pine (*Pandanus* spp.) Suckers.

Sea onion (*Ornithogalum caudatum*) Bulblets.

Shrimp plant (*Justicia Brandegeana*) Stem cuttings.

Snake plant (*Sansevieria trifasciata*) Division; cross sections of leaves.

Spanish-shawl (*Heterocentron elegans*) Stem cuttings.

Spider lily (*Hymenocallis* spp.) Seeds; bulblets.

Spider plant (*Chlorophytum comosum*) Root plantlets at leaf tips; division when repotting.

Star jasmine (*Trachelospermum jasminoides*) Stem cuttings.

Strawberry geranium (*Saxifraga stolonifera*) Fasten plantlets at tip of runners on moist soil.

Streptocarpus (*Streptocarpus* spp.) Seeds; leaf cuttings; leaf sections.

Sundew (*Drosera* spp.) Seeds; division.

Swedish ivy (*Plectranthus australis*) Stem cuttings. (W)

Sweet flag (*Acorus gramineus* 'Variegatus') Division of rootstock. (W)

Sweet-potato vine (*Ipomoea Batatas*) Stem cuttings; division of tubers but include an "eye."

Tahitian bridal veil (*Gibasis geniculata*) Stem cuttings. (W)

Temple-bells (*Smithiantha* spp.) Seeds; rhizome cuttings; leaf cuttings without the petiole.

Thanksgiving cactus (*Schlumbergera truncatus*) Leaf joints.

Ti plant (*Cordyline terminalis*) Air layer; stem sections; root sections. (W)

Umbrella plant (*Cyperus alternifolius*) Seeds; division; tip cuttings. (W)

Velvet plant (*Gynura aurantiaca*) Stem cuttings. (W)

Venus's-flytrap (*Dionaea muscipula*) Seeds; division; leaf cuttings.

Walking iris (*Neomarica gracilis*) Division; root plantlets at end of leaves.

Wandering Jew (*Zebrina* spp.) Stem cuttings. (W)

Watsonia (*Watsonia* spp.) Bulblets.

Wood rose (*Merremia tuberosa*) Seeds, but notch seed coat before sowing; stem cuttings.

Zebra plant (*Aphelandra* spp.) Seeds; stem cuttings in spring at 70°F (21°C).

Zebra plant (*Calathea zebrina*) Division when repotting.

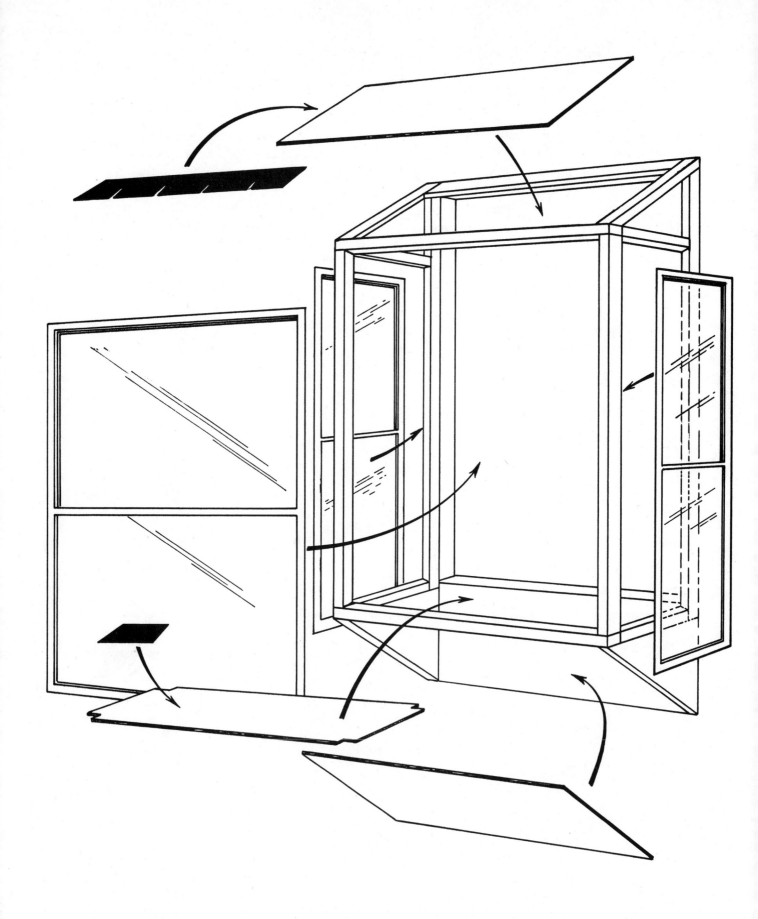

Appendix D: A Greenhouse Window

The greenhouse window that I mentioned in the introduction was made from aluminum storm windows purchased at the local lumberyard. It was designed to fit an opening in the outer wall of the front room that originally held a large wooden window with two frames of the old-fashioned type that used clothesline and lead weights, and that had wavy panes in evidence of the great age of the glass.

The roof on the new greenhouse was shingled instead of using glass, since the winter sun is so low in the sky we knew we could do without the extra light. The affair projected eighteen inches out into the air, the two sides closed with narrower aluminum storm windows. The greenhouse floor was made of marine plywood that I covered with black vinyl slate. Two sheets of acrylic in wooden frames were hinged to the inside of the frame and closed the greenhouse to the room during the winter. Finally, the electrician installed an outlet under the window, and I bought a small electric heater.

The screens that come with aluminum storm windows provide adequate ventilation in the summer and also help cut summer sunlight for sensitive plants.

The materials used were:

4 white aluminum storm windows
¾-inch AA plywood (exterior grade)
Standard two-by-fours
Standard one-by-twos
Roof shingling

◀ The drawing on the opposite page shows the construction of a window greenhouse. The framing is made of standard two-by-fours. The bottom, the flooring, and the roof are of AA plywood (exterior grade); the roof is then shingled. The windows are standard white enamel, aluminum storm windows.

Appendix E: Bibliography

Bailey, L. H. *How Plants Get Their Names*. New York: Dover Publications, Inc., 1963. A reprint of the 1933 edition of a marvelous book that deals with botanical nomenclature.

————. *Hortus Second*. New York: The Macmillan Company, 1941. The second Hortus and just as valuable for what it omits as for what it includes.

Coats, Alice M. *The Plant Hunters*. New York: McGraw-Hill Book Company, 1969. A history of the horticultural pioneers, including their plant discoveries from the Renaissance to the twentieth century.

Dictionary of Gardening. The Royal Horticultural Society. 4 vols. and supplement. Oxford: Clarendon, 1965. Next to *Hortus Third* and the *Exotic Plant Manual*, these volumes are the most used in my library. Fascinating not only for advice on plants and planting, but for garden history, too.

Elbert, George A., and Virginie F. Elbert. *Foliage Plants for Decorating Indoors*. Portland, Oregon: Timber Press, 1989. A new compendium of pictures and information on plants usually grown for their interesting or attractive foliage with much information on artificial light.

Graf, Alfred Byrd. *Exotic Plant Manual*. East Rutherford, New Jersey: Roehrs Company, 1970. Thousands of pictures of indoor plants and advice on growing by one of the leaders in the horticultural industry.

Hortus Third. New York: Macmillan, 1976. This is the monumental revision of L. H. Bailey and Ethel Zoe Bailey's original work of nomenclature for the American gardener and horticulturist, overseen by the staff of the L. H. Bailey Hortorium at Cornell University.

Indoor Gardening. Brooklyn, New York: Brooklyn Botanic Garden, 1987. Another book in the excellent series, Plants & Gardens, that deals with all aspects of indoor gardening from plant selection to growing under lights.

Jervis, Roy N. *Aglaonema Grower's Notebook*. Clearwater, Florida, privately printed.

Loewer, Peter. *Bringing the Outdoors In*. Chicago/New York: Contemporary Books, 1988. A reprint of a 1974 book about indoor gardening.

Martin, Tovah. *Once upon a Windowsill*. Portland, Oregon: Timber Press, 1988. A charming history of growing plants indoors and the world of houseplant fashion.

Menninger, Edwin A. *Flowering Vines of the World*. New York: Hearthside Press Inc., 1970. An encyclopedic book on flowering vines.

Perry, Frances. *Flowers of the World*. London: The Hamlyn Publishing Group Ltd., 1972. Distributed by Crown Publishers, Inc. A beautifully illustrated book that includes a great deal of history about plants.

PART SEVEN

INDEX

Bold type denotes illustration

A

If you enjoyed *The Indoor Window Garden*, try this popular gardening classic that is available in your local bookstore or by mail. To order directly, return the coupon below with payment to: Best Publications, Department BSD, 180 North Michigan Avenue, Chicago, Illinois 60601. Or call (312) 782-9181 to order with your credit card.

- -

Qty.	Title/Author	Price	Total
____	*Glorious Gardens: A Portfolio of Ideas for Planting & Design* by Francesca Greenoak (0207-9Z)	$29.95 ea.	$_____
	Subtotal		$_____

Add $2.50 postage for the first book ordered. $__2.50__

Add $1.00 postage for each additional book ordered. $_____

Illinois residents add 7% sales tax;
California residents add 6% sales tax. $_____

Total Price $_____

Name _____

Address _____

City/State/Zip _____

☐ Enclosed is my check/money order payable to Best Publications.

Bill my

☐ VISA   Account No. _____

☐ MasterCard   Expiration Date _____

Signature _____

For quantity discount information, please call the sales department at (312) 782-9181. Allow four to six weeks for delivery.

Offer expires June 30, 1991.   IN0690

A-1